This book belongs to the extraordinary
_____,
whose a brilliance and creativity fill our hearts with pride and admiration with every colorful stroke. May his journey be as vibrant and inspiring as the colors he chooses to paint the world.

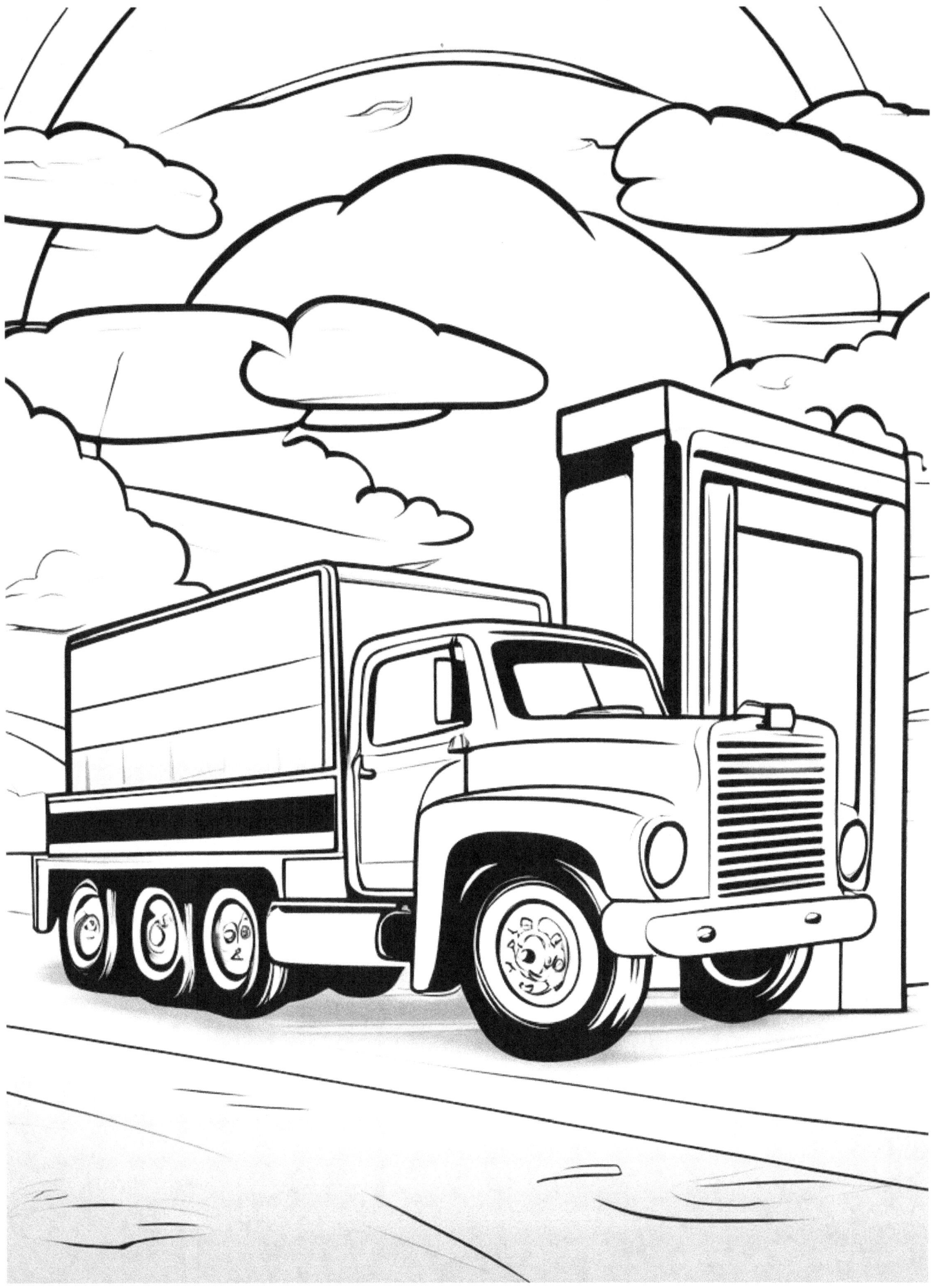

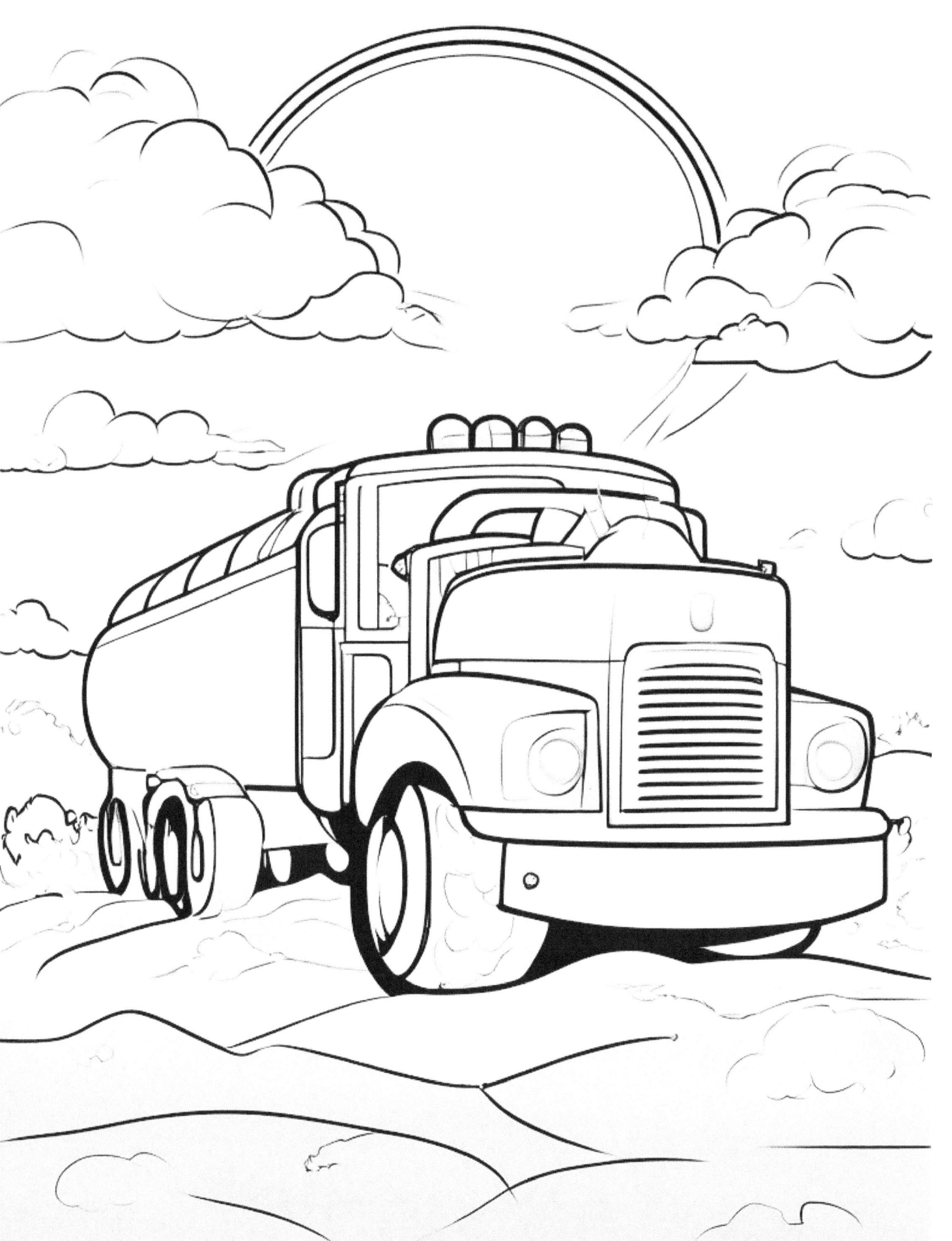

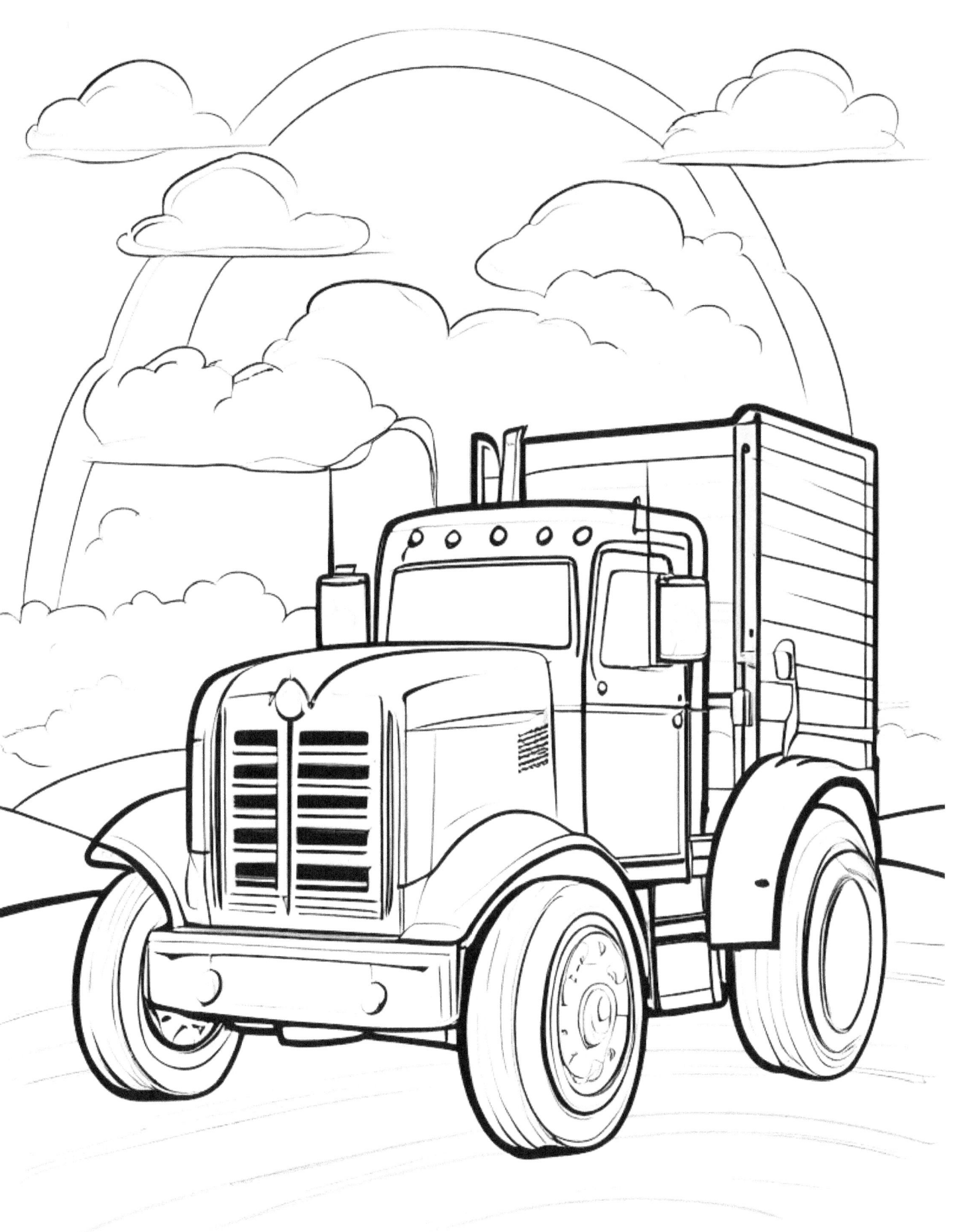

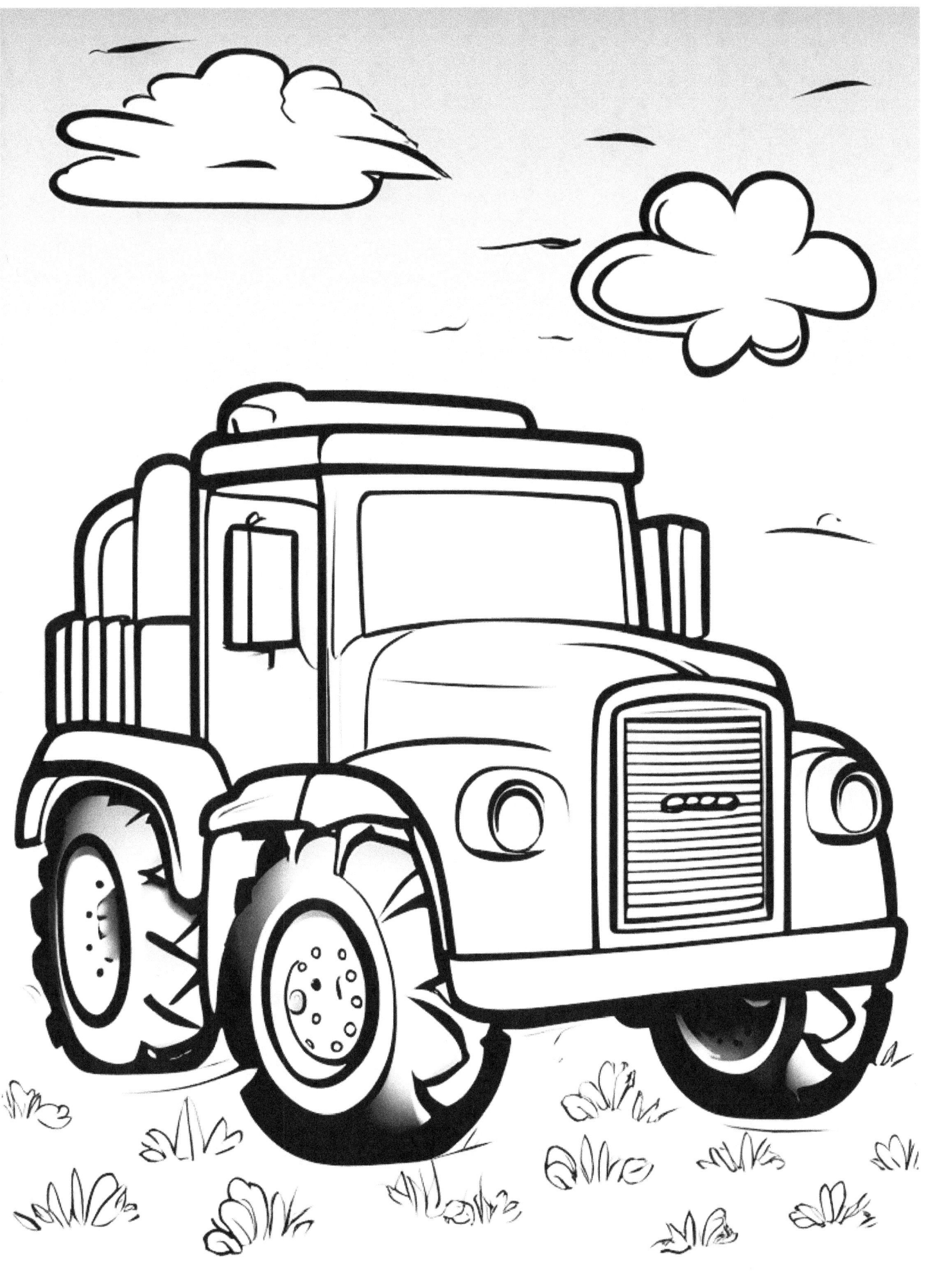

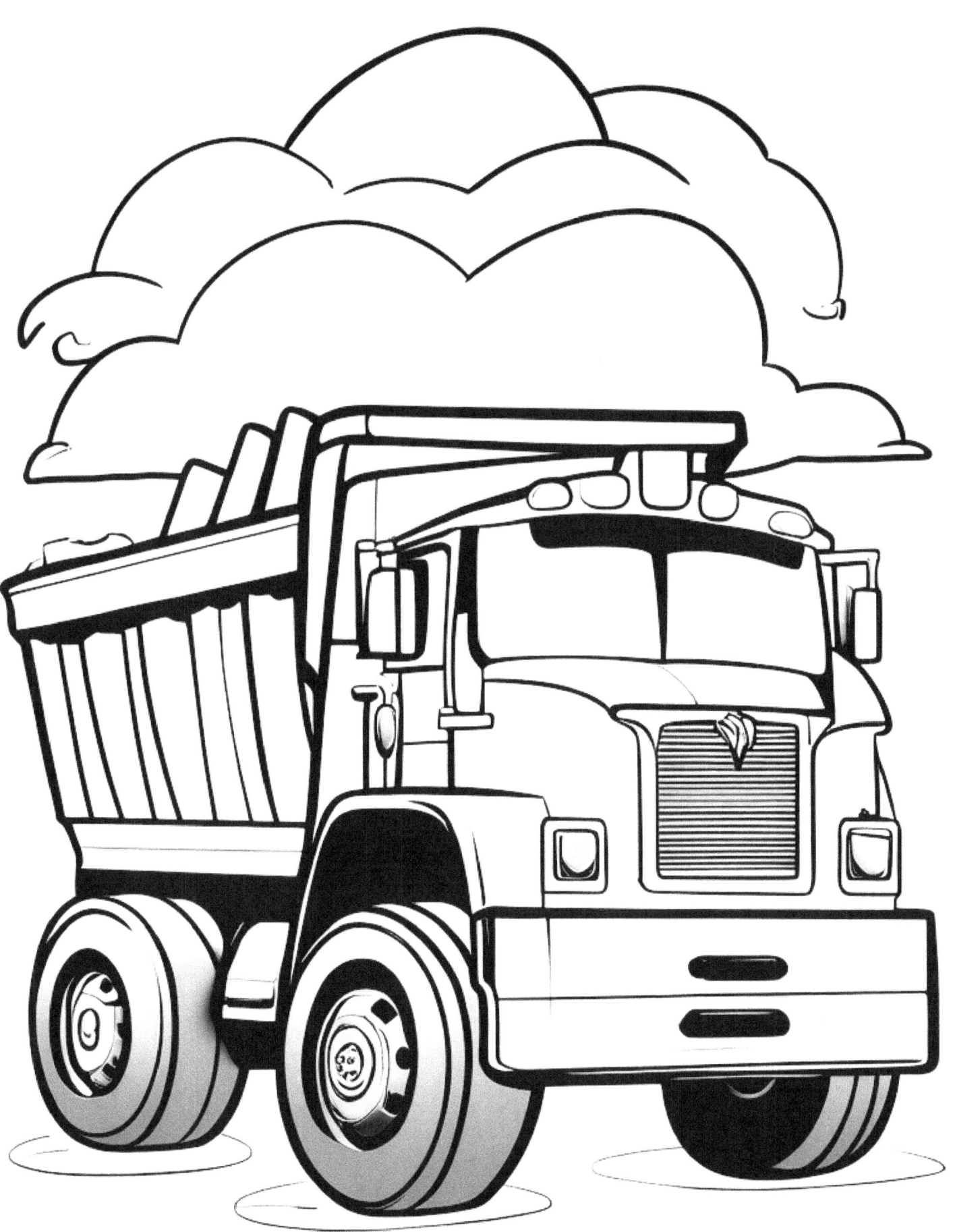

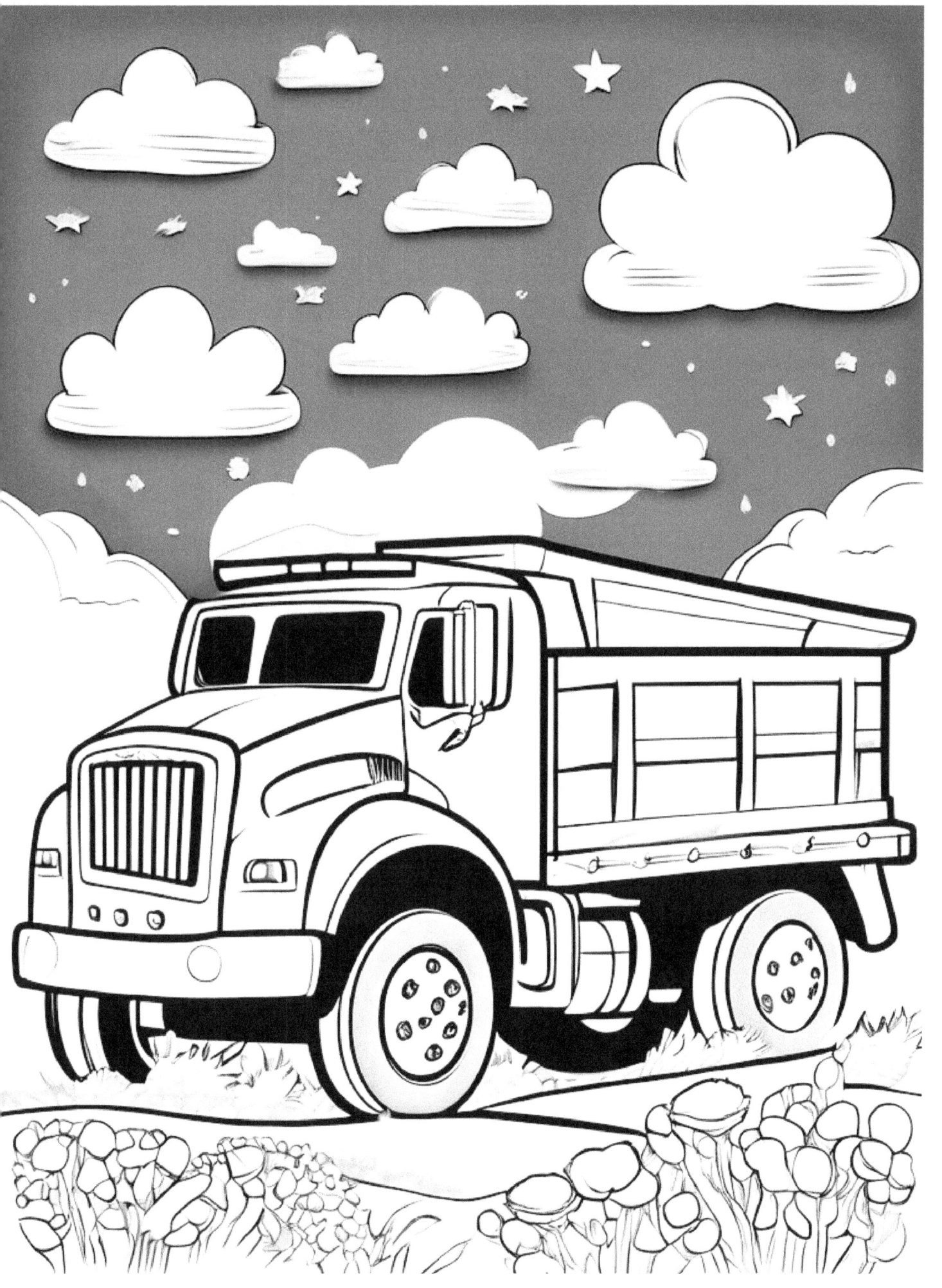

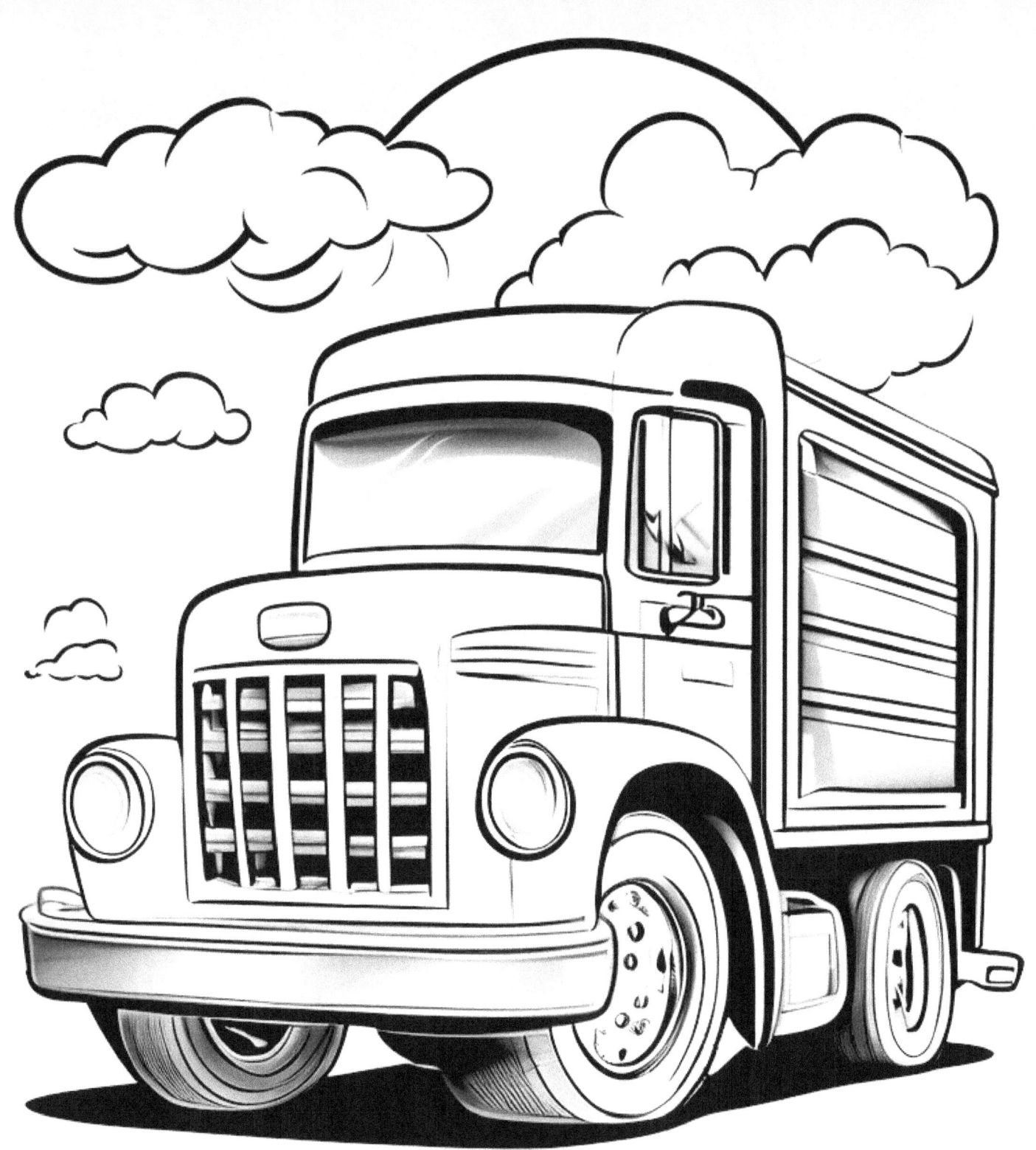

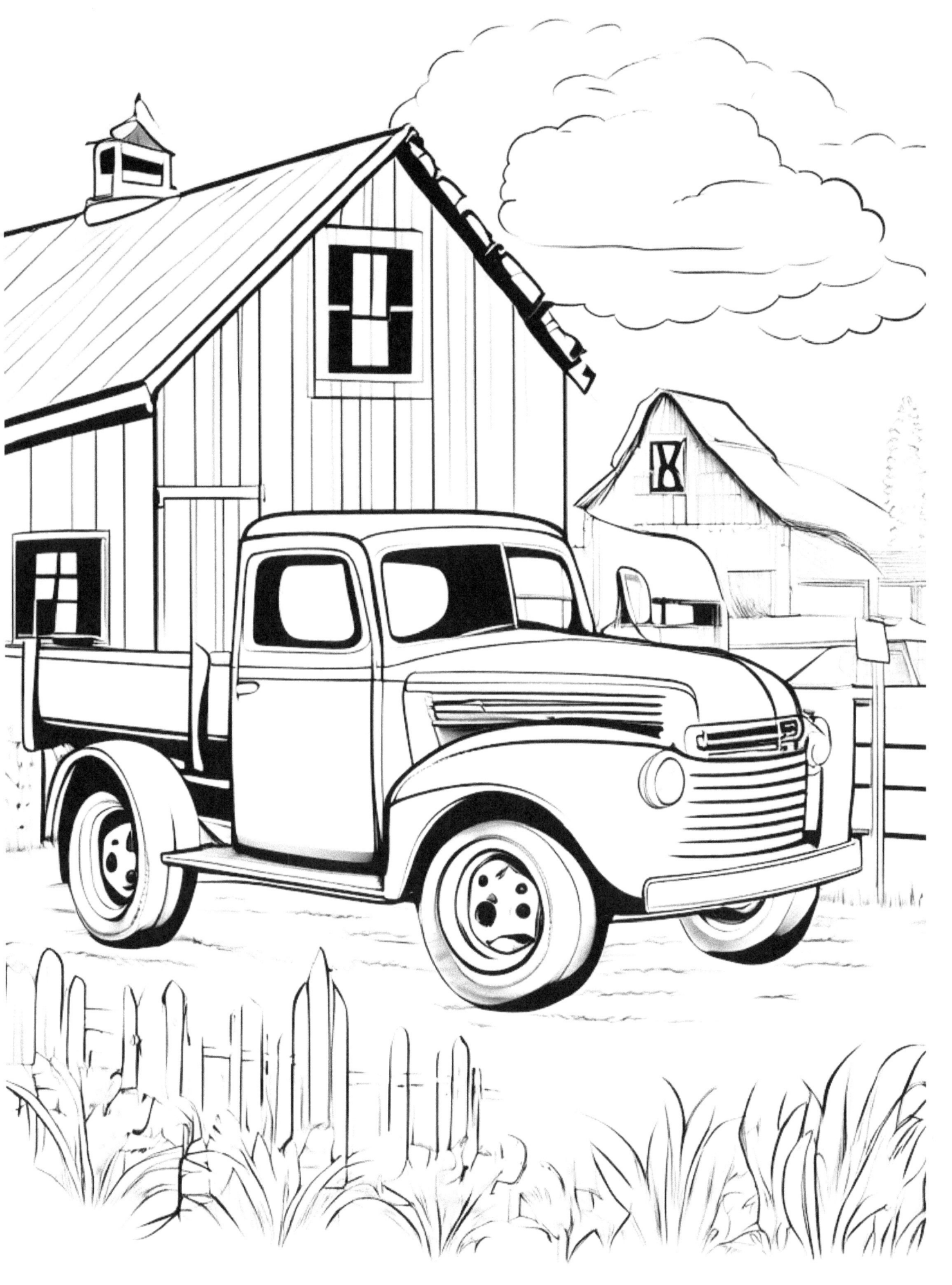

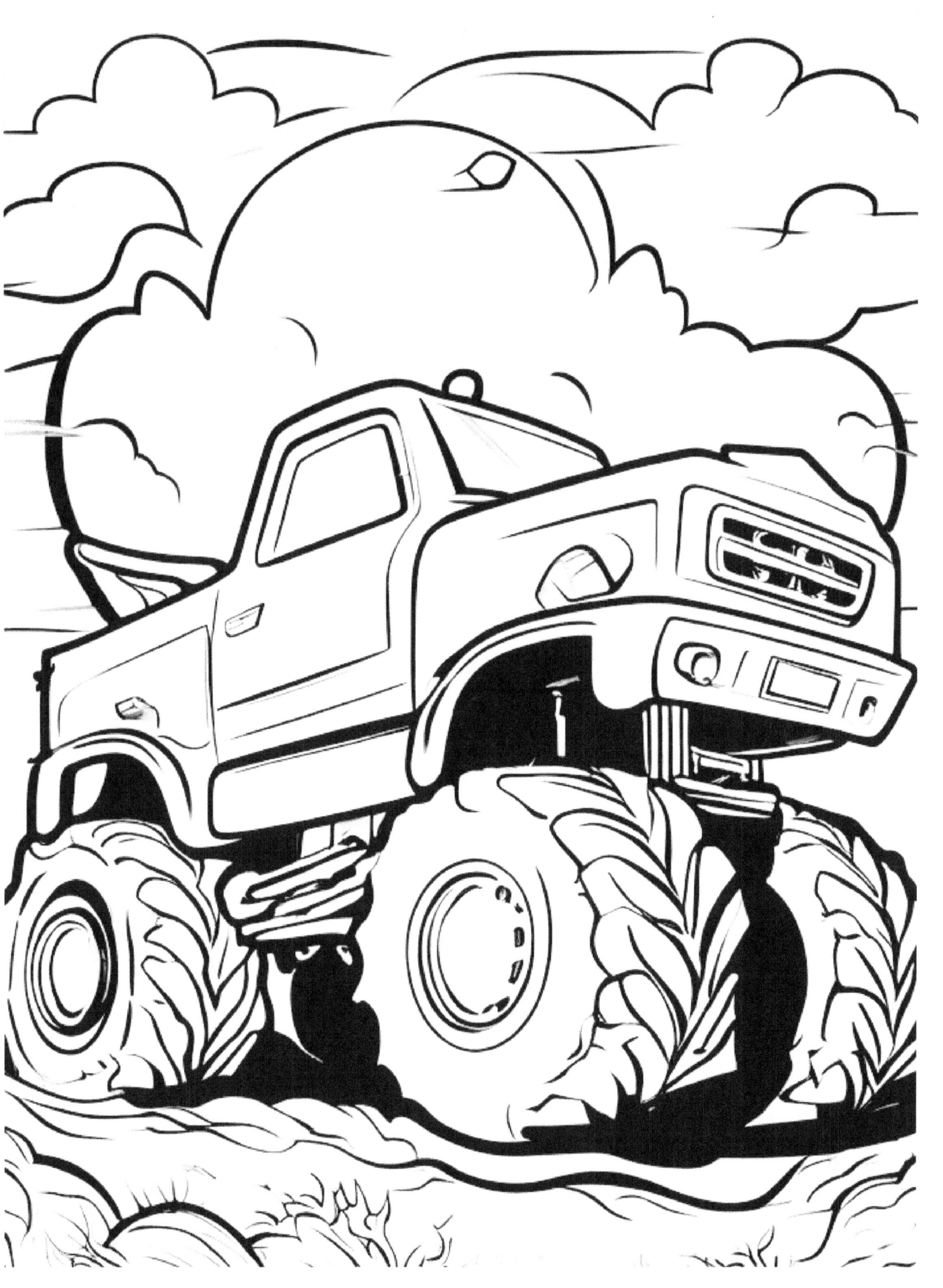

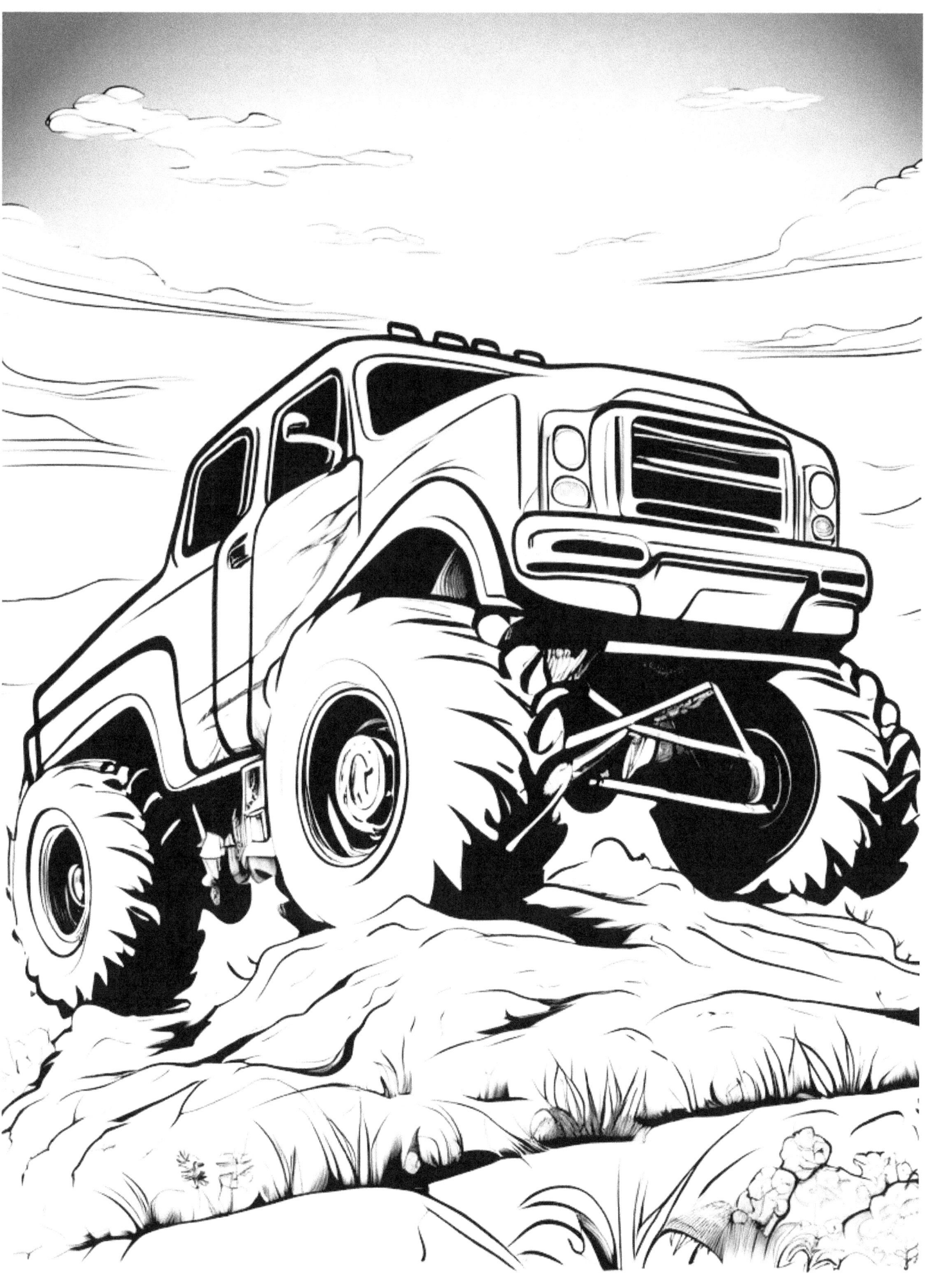

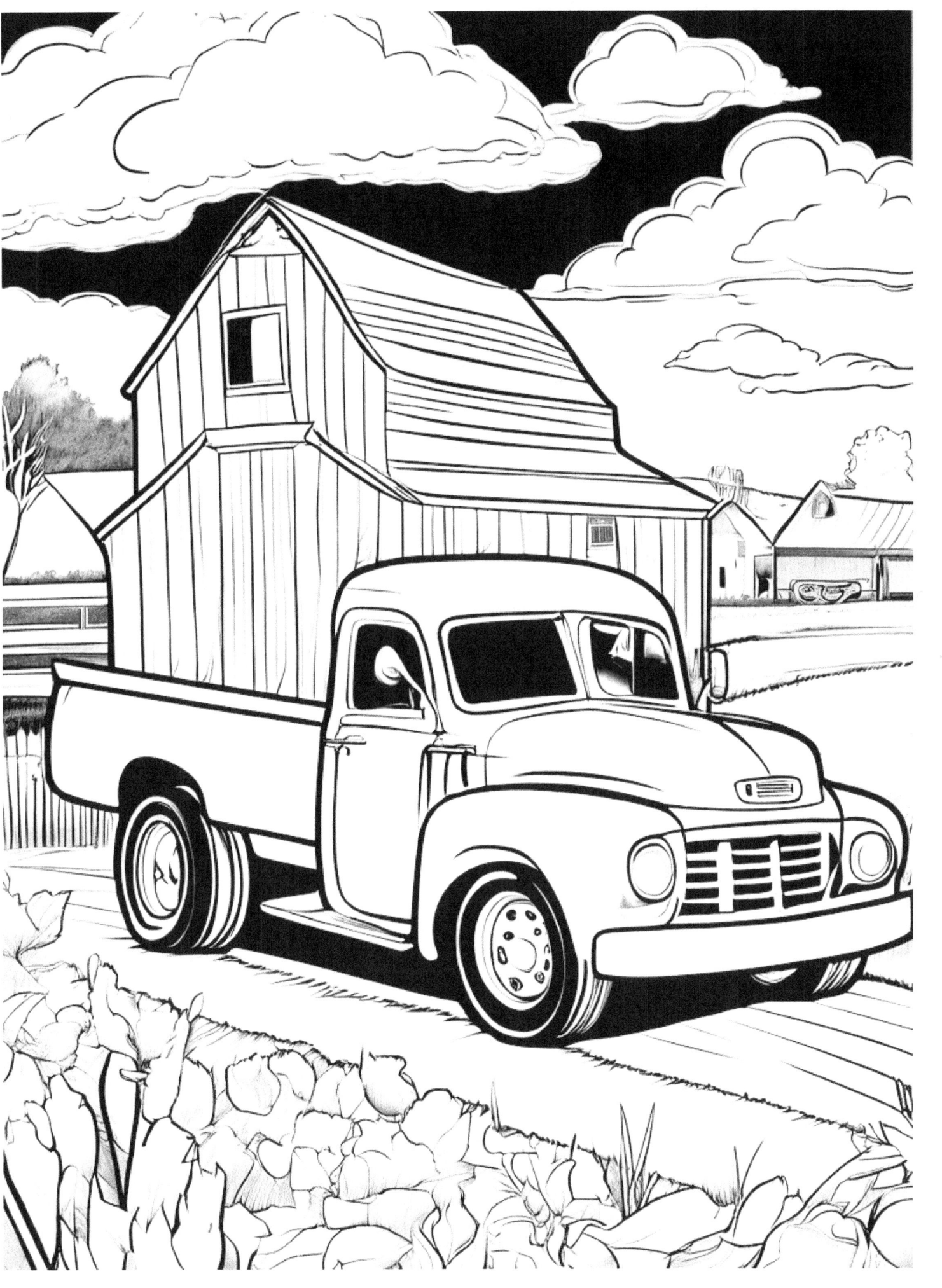

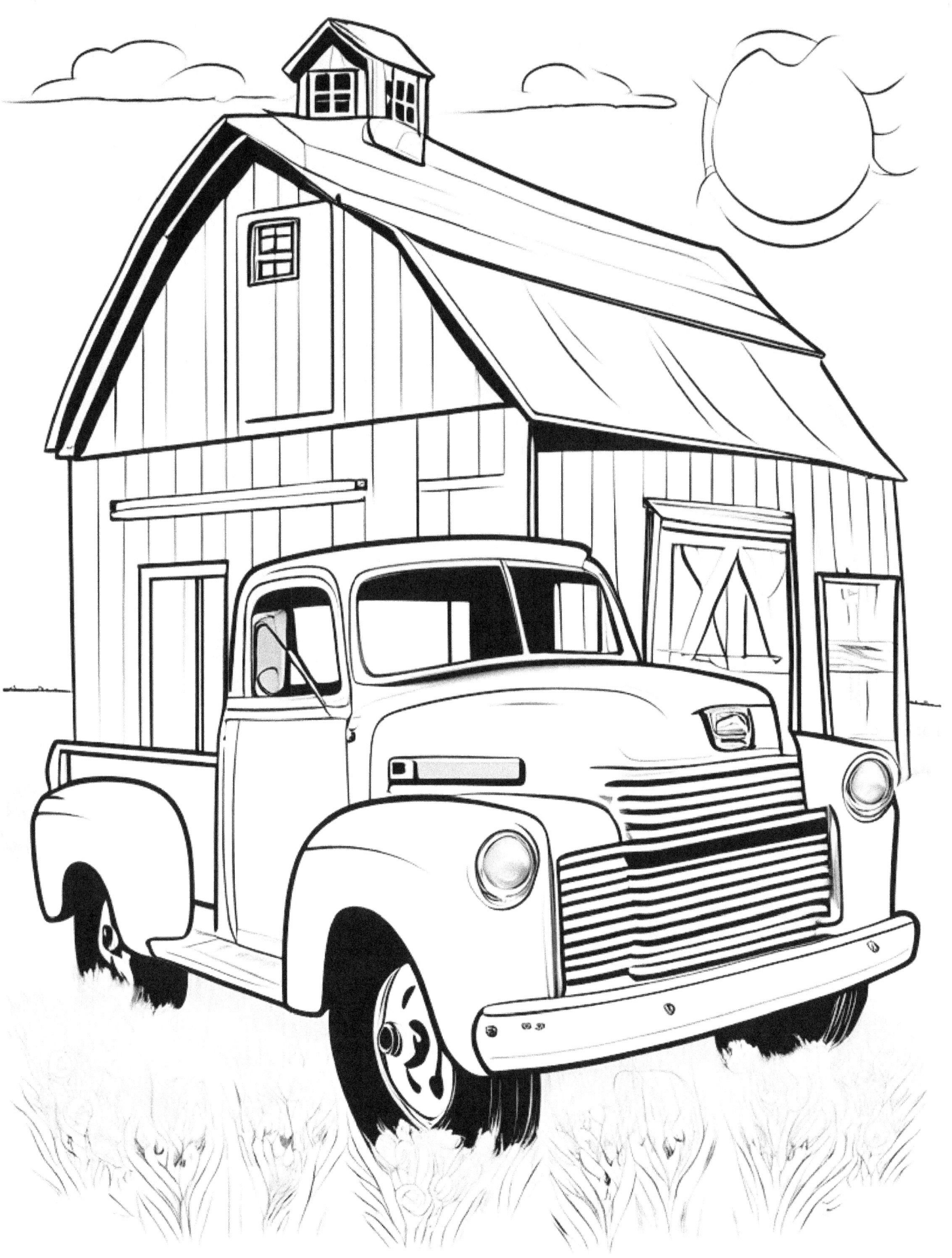

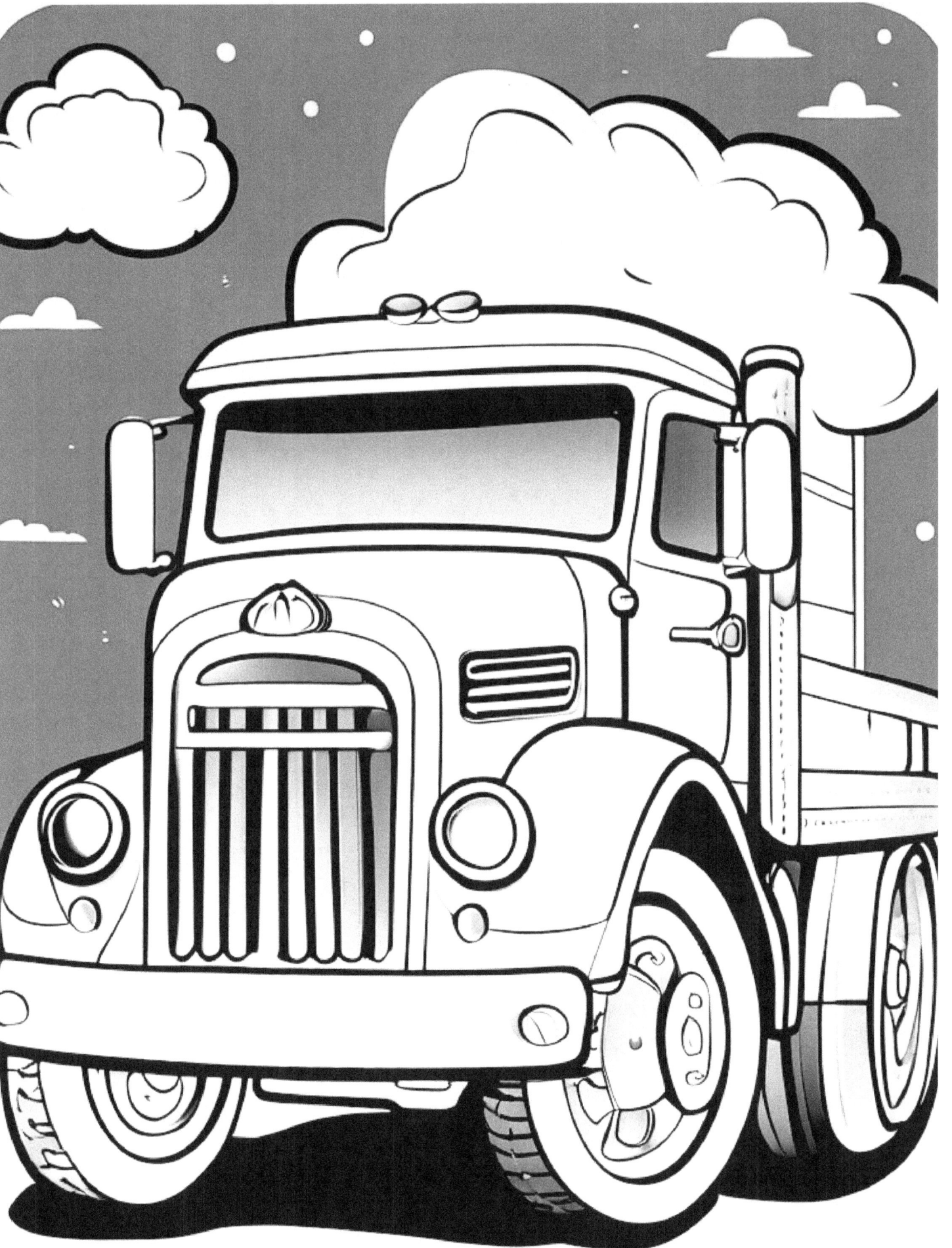

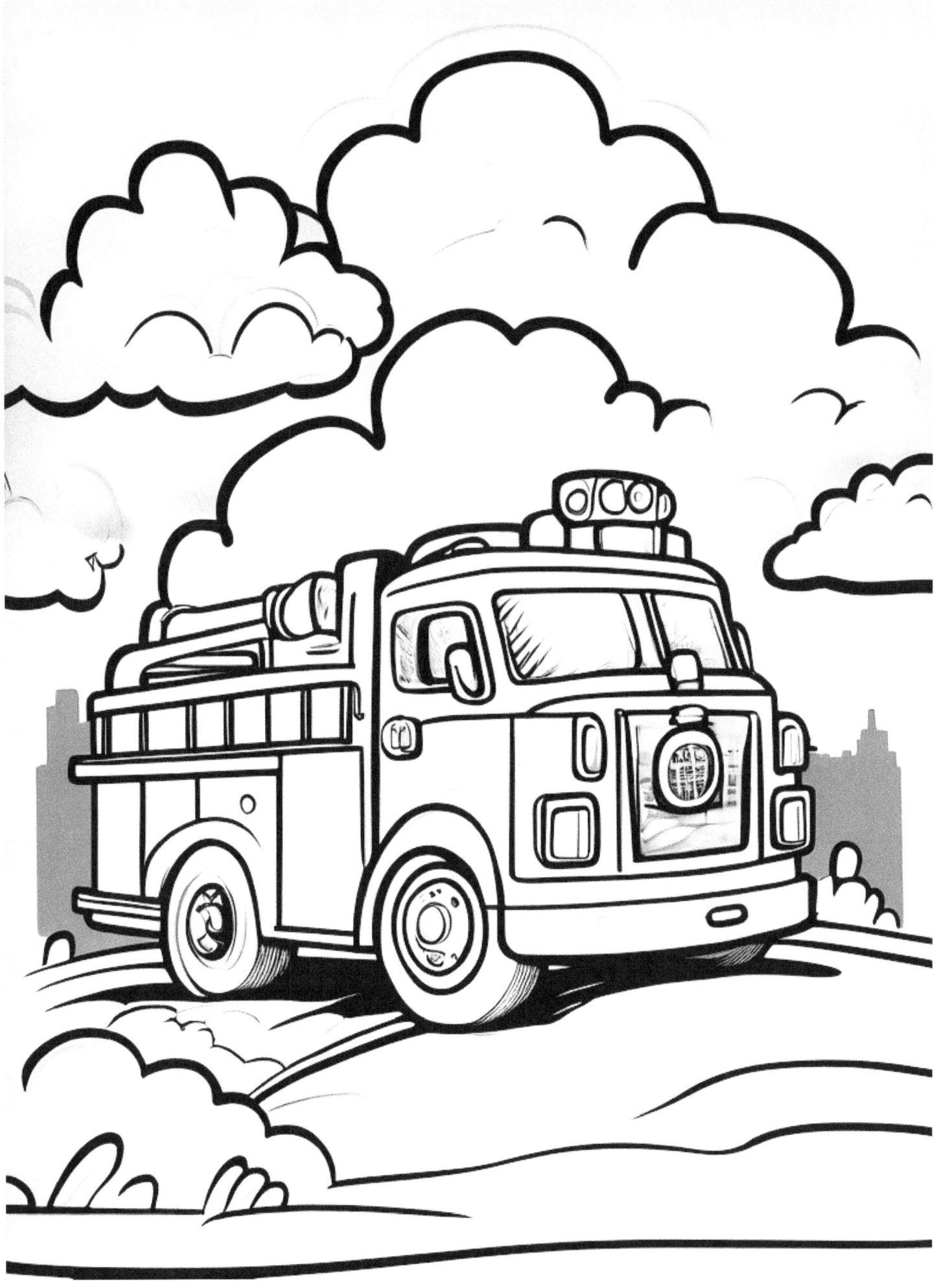

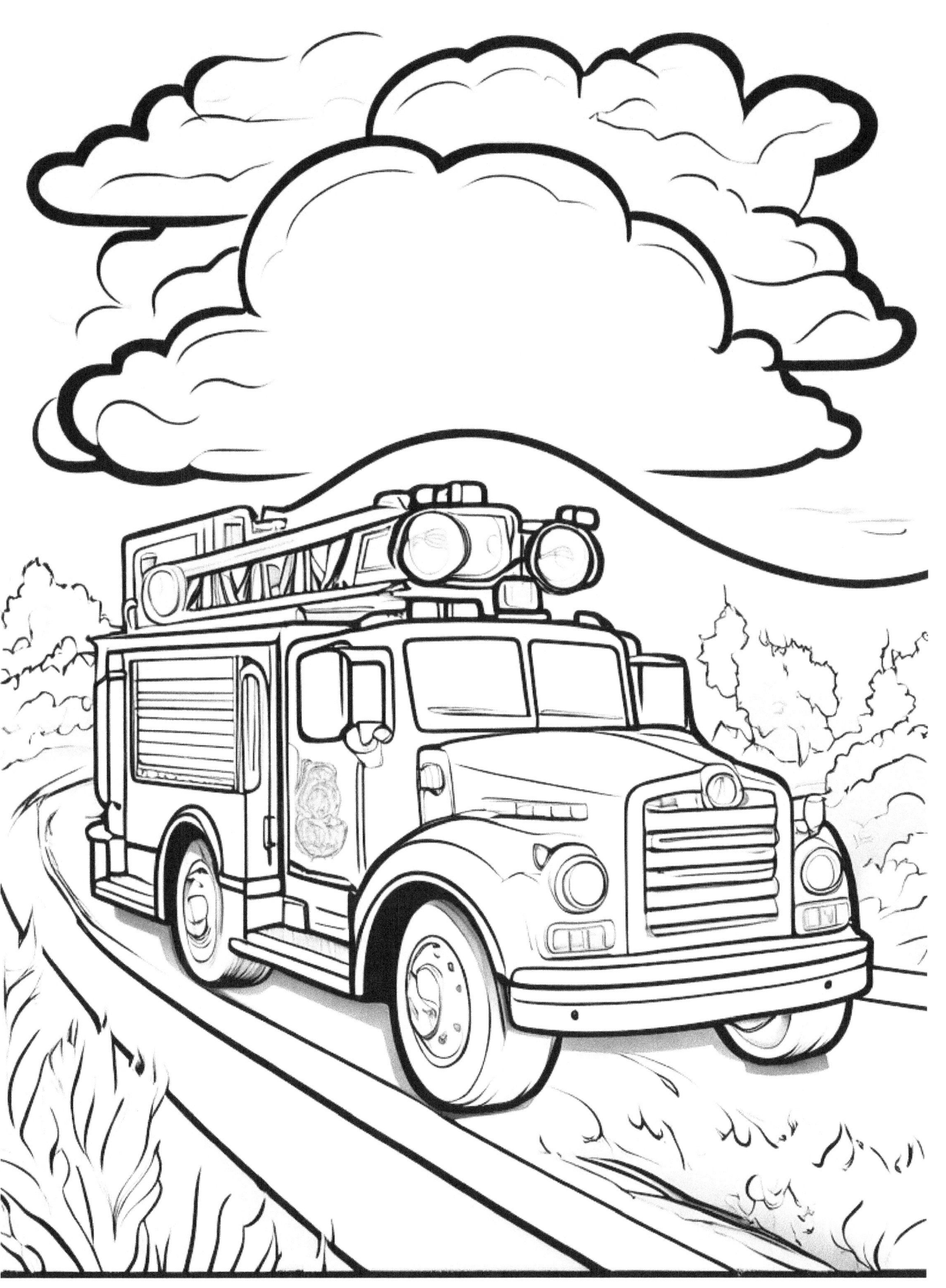

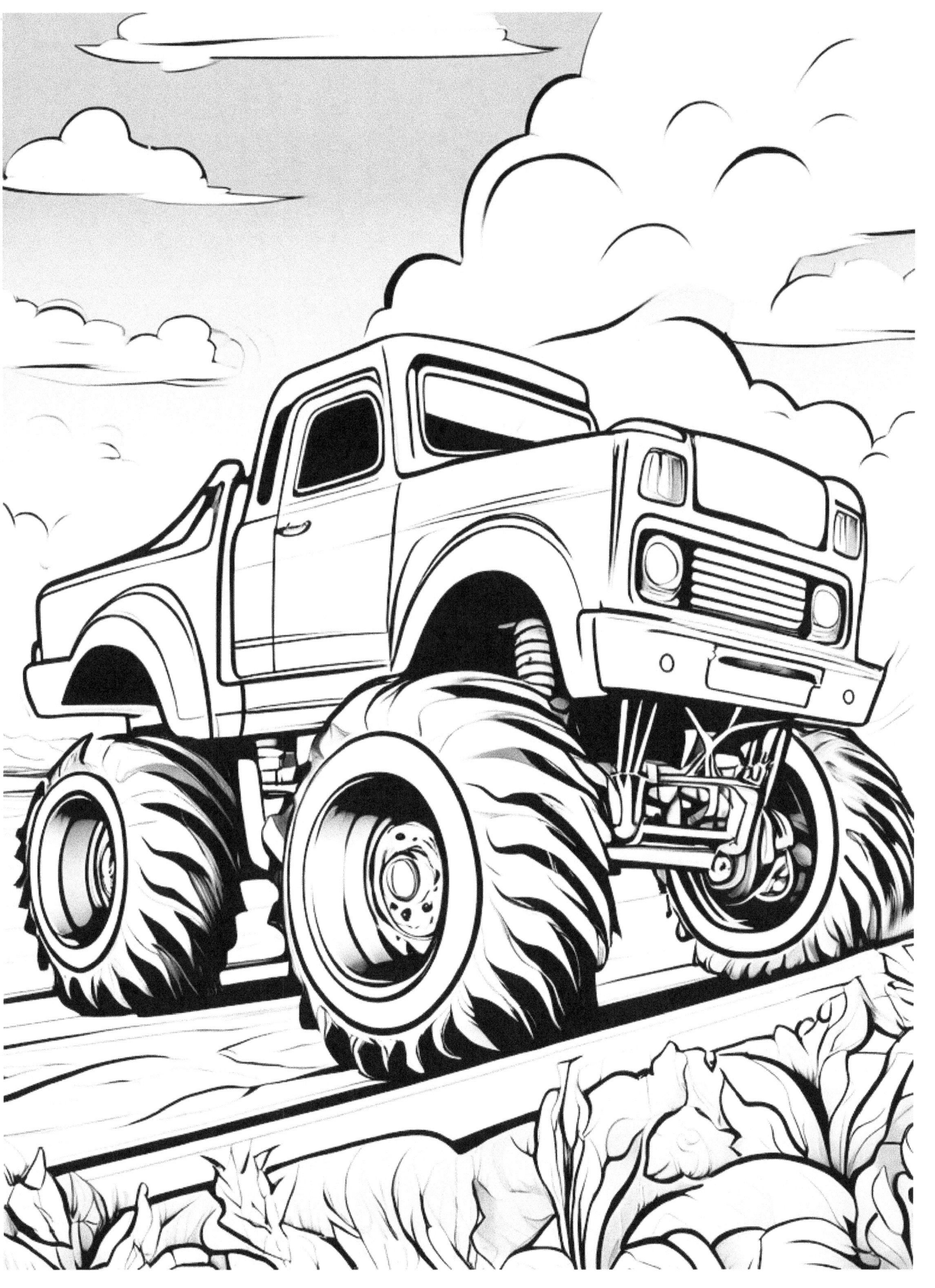

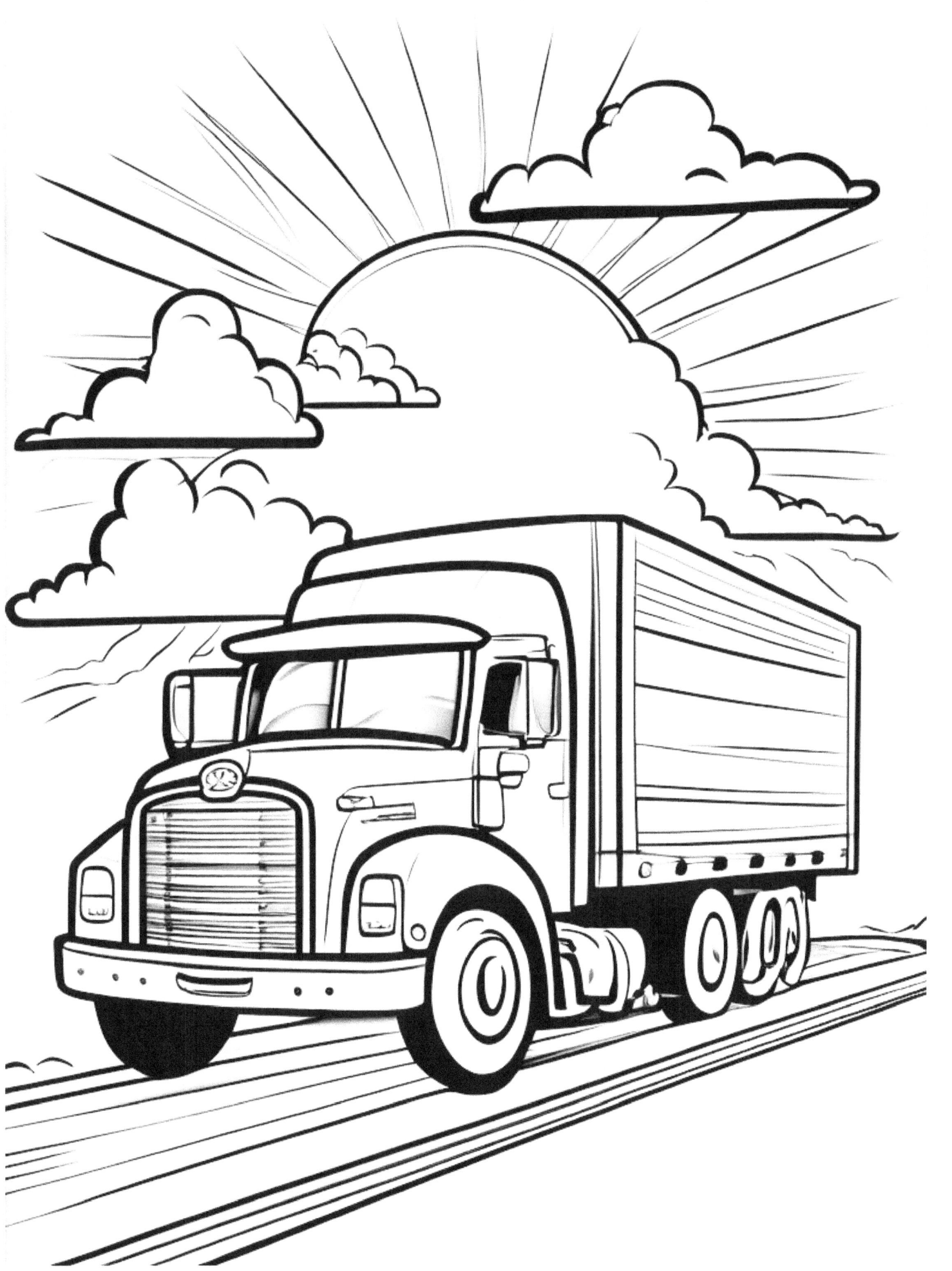

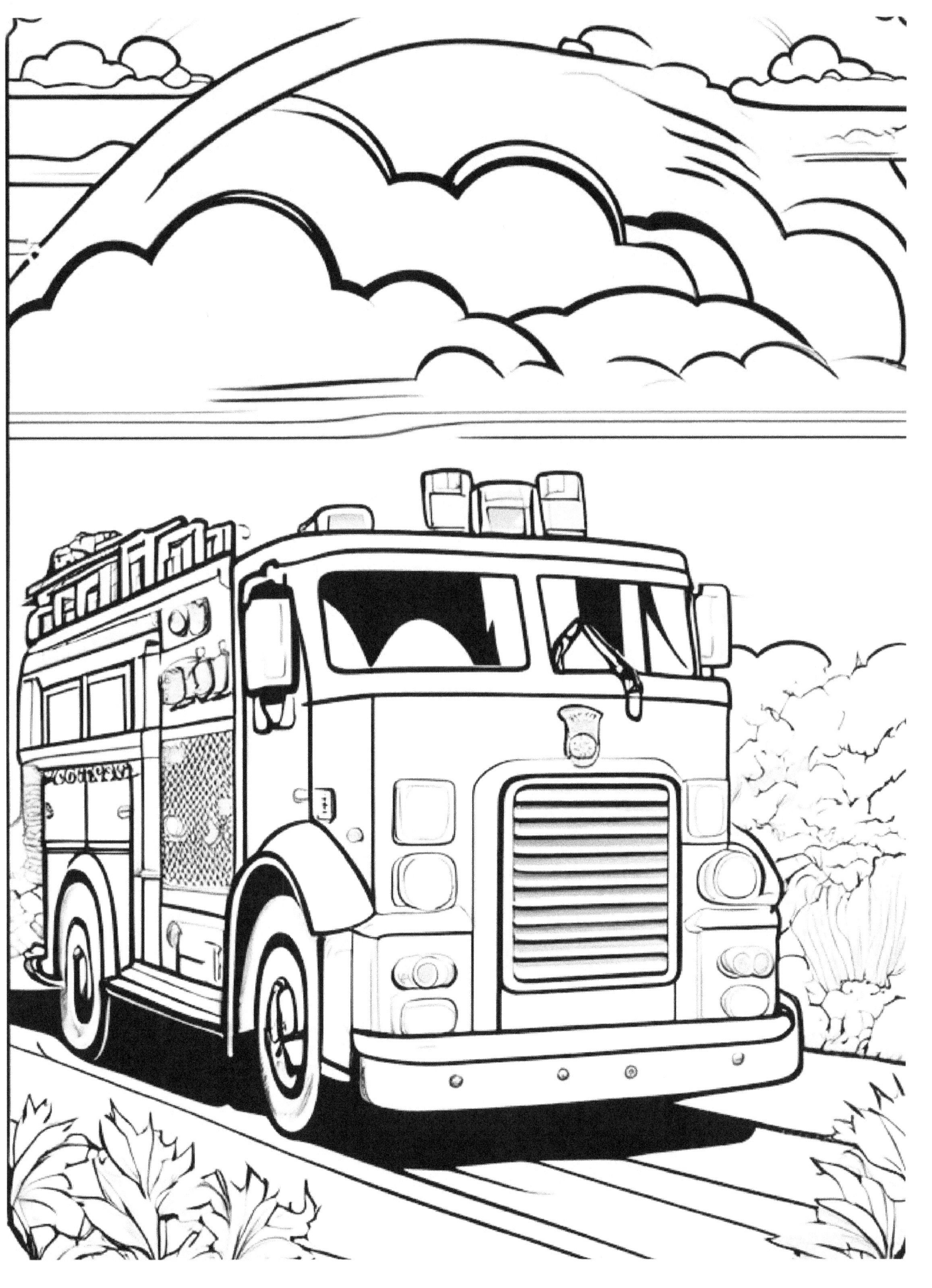

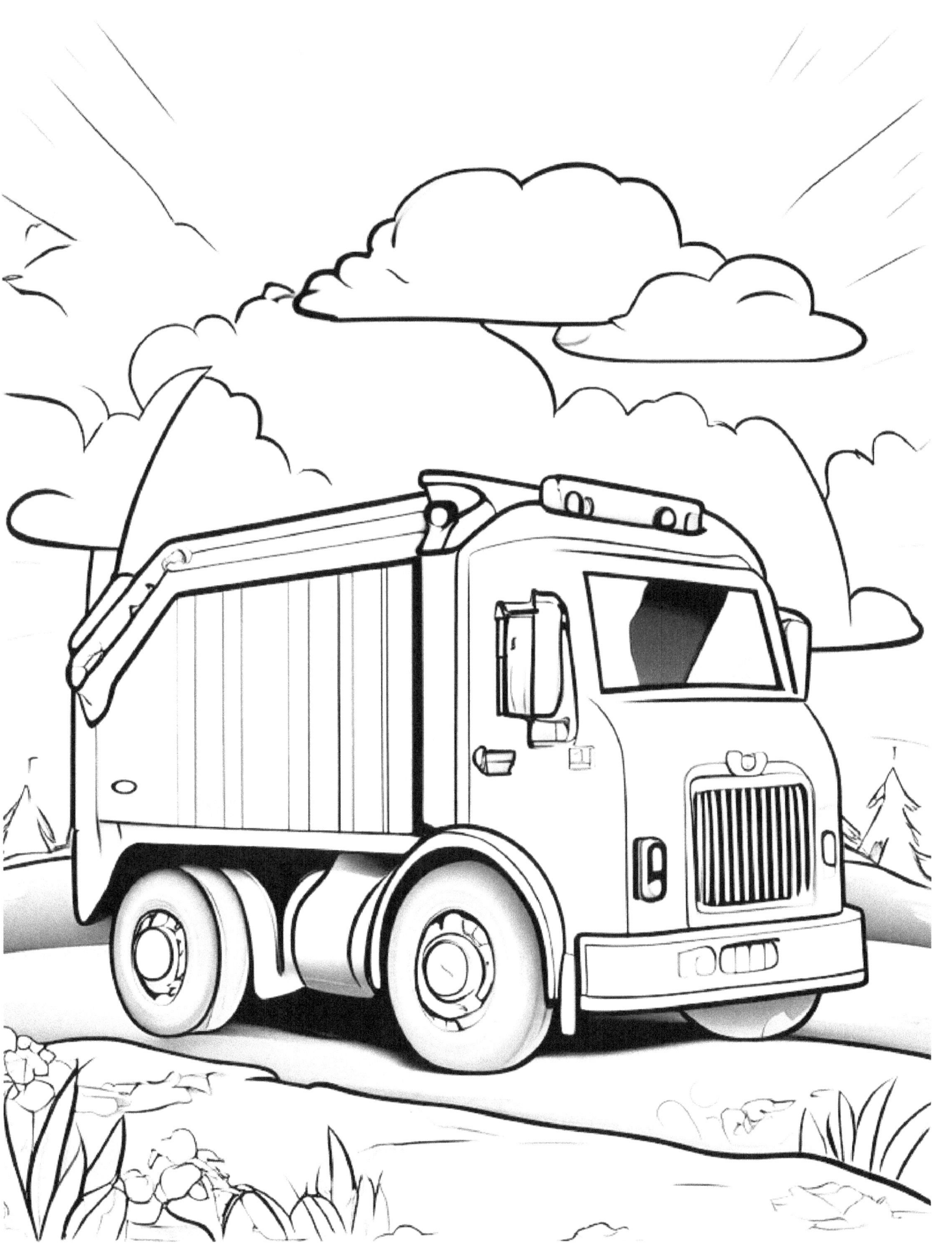

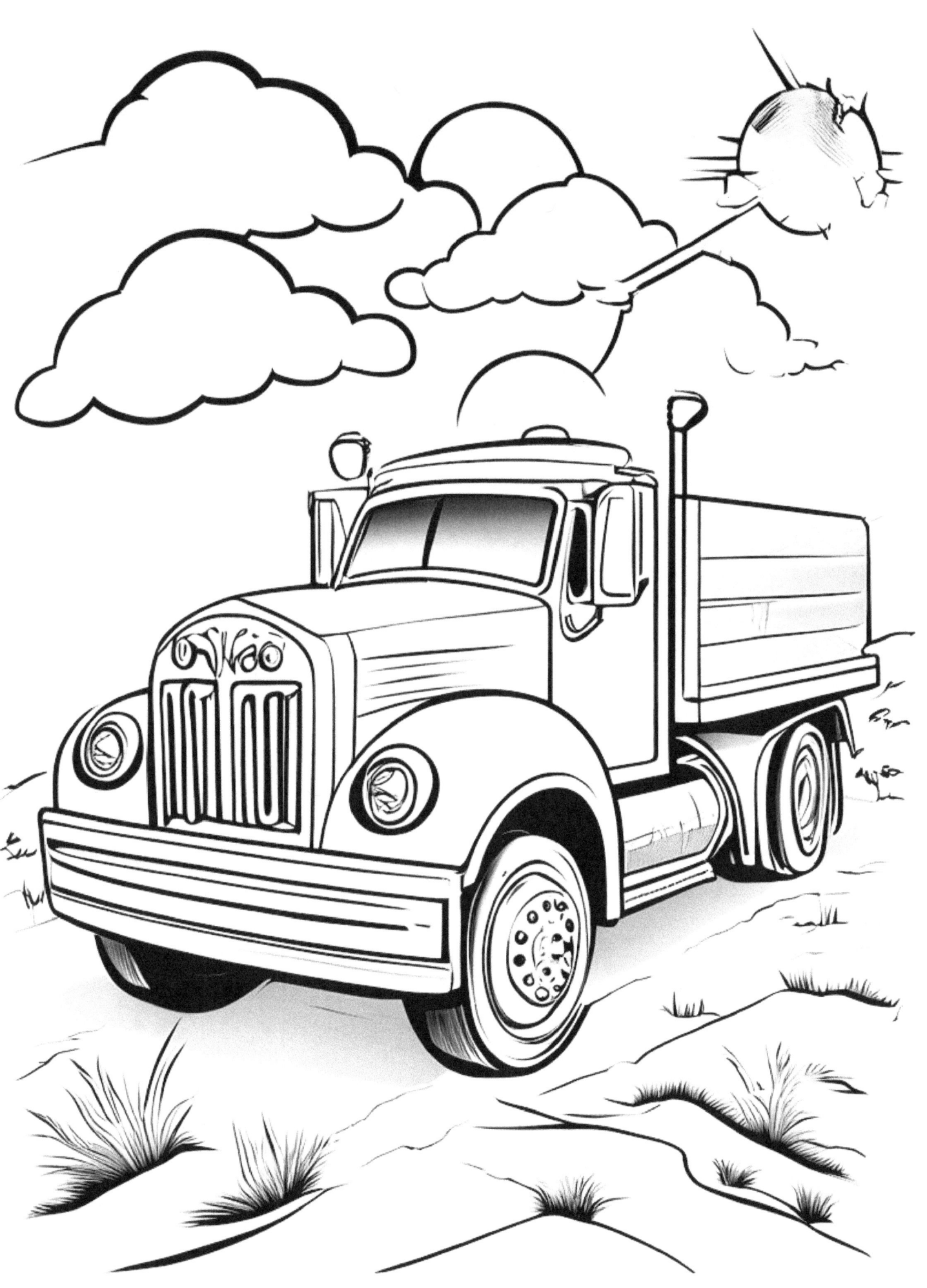

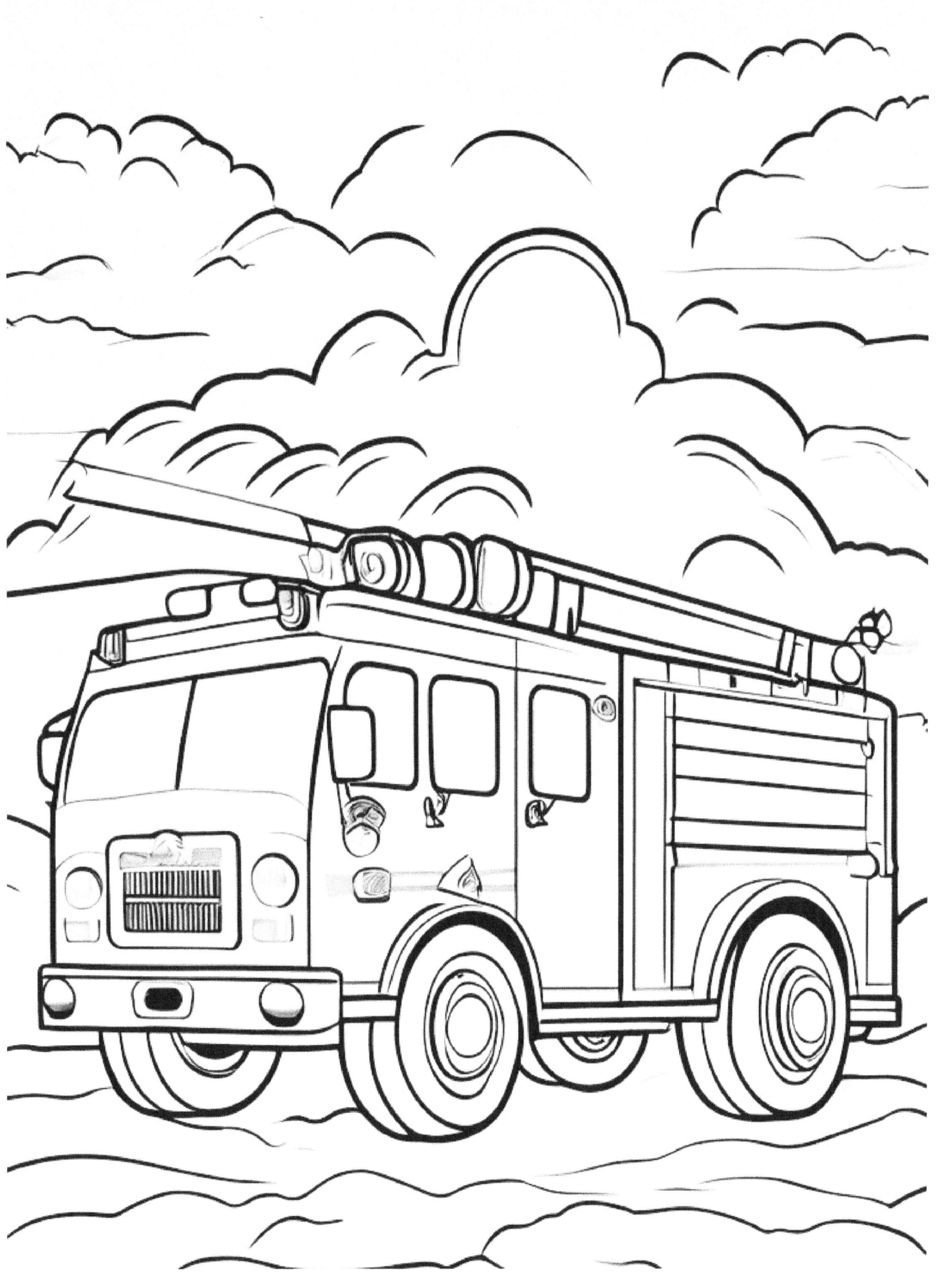

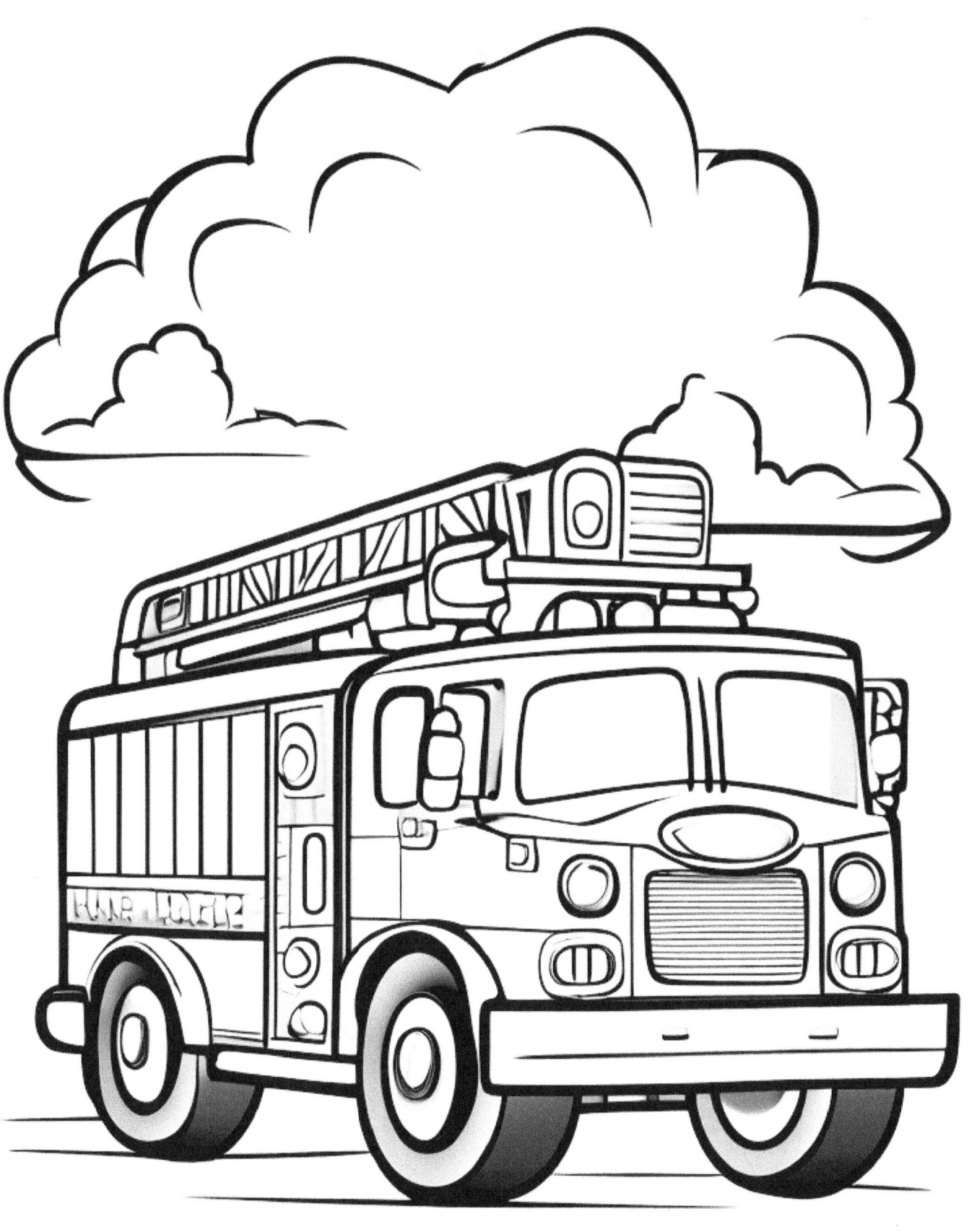

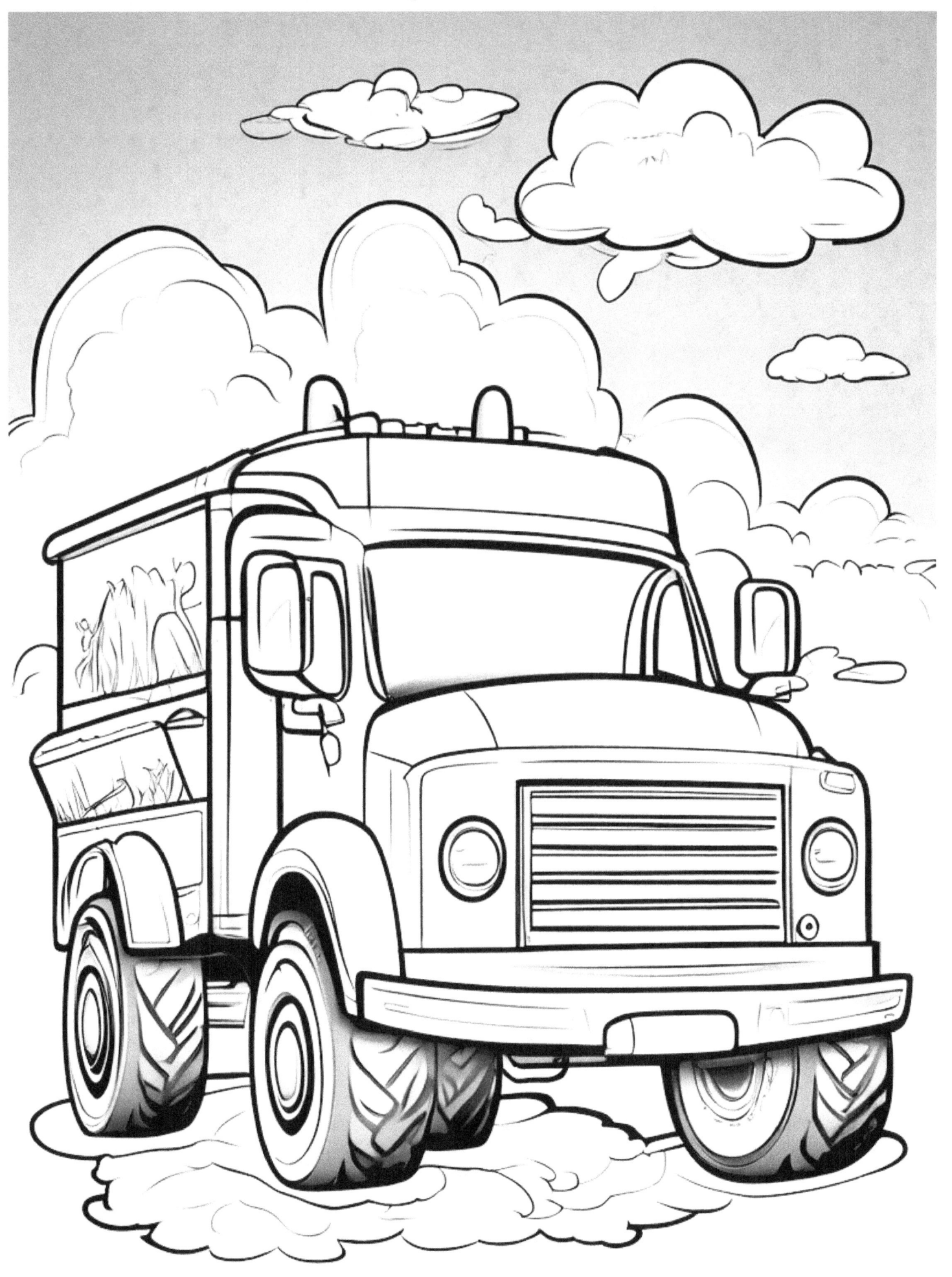

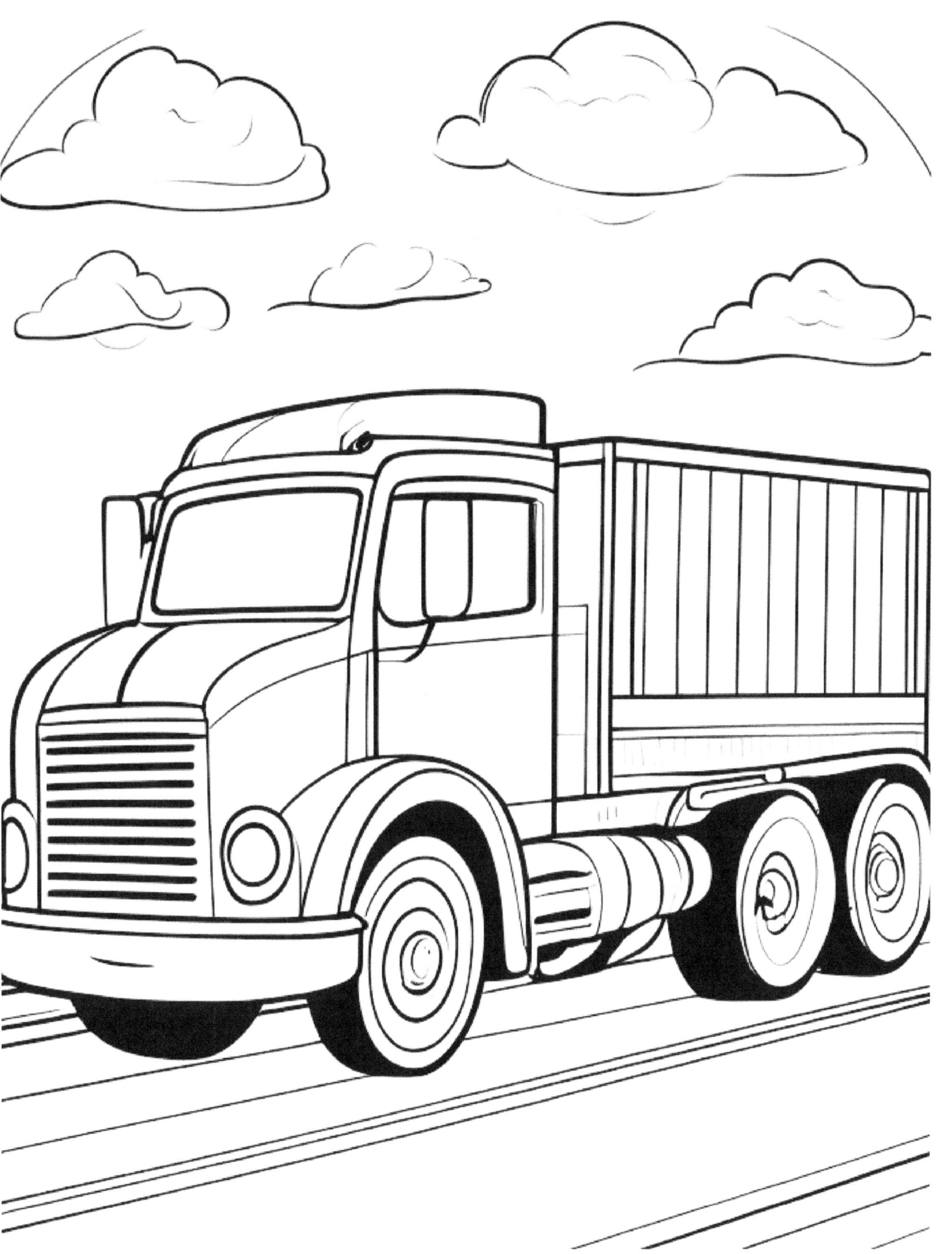

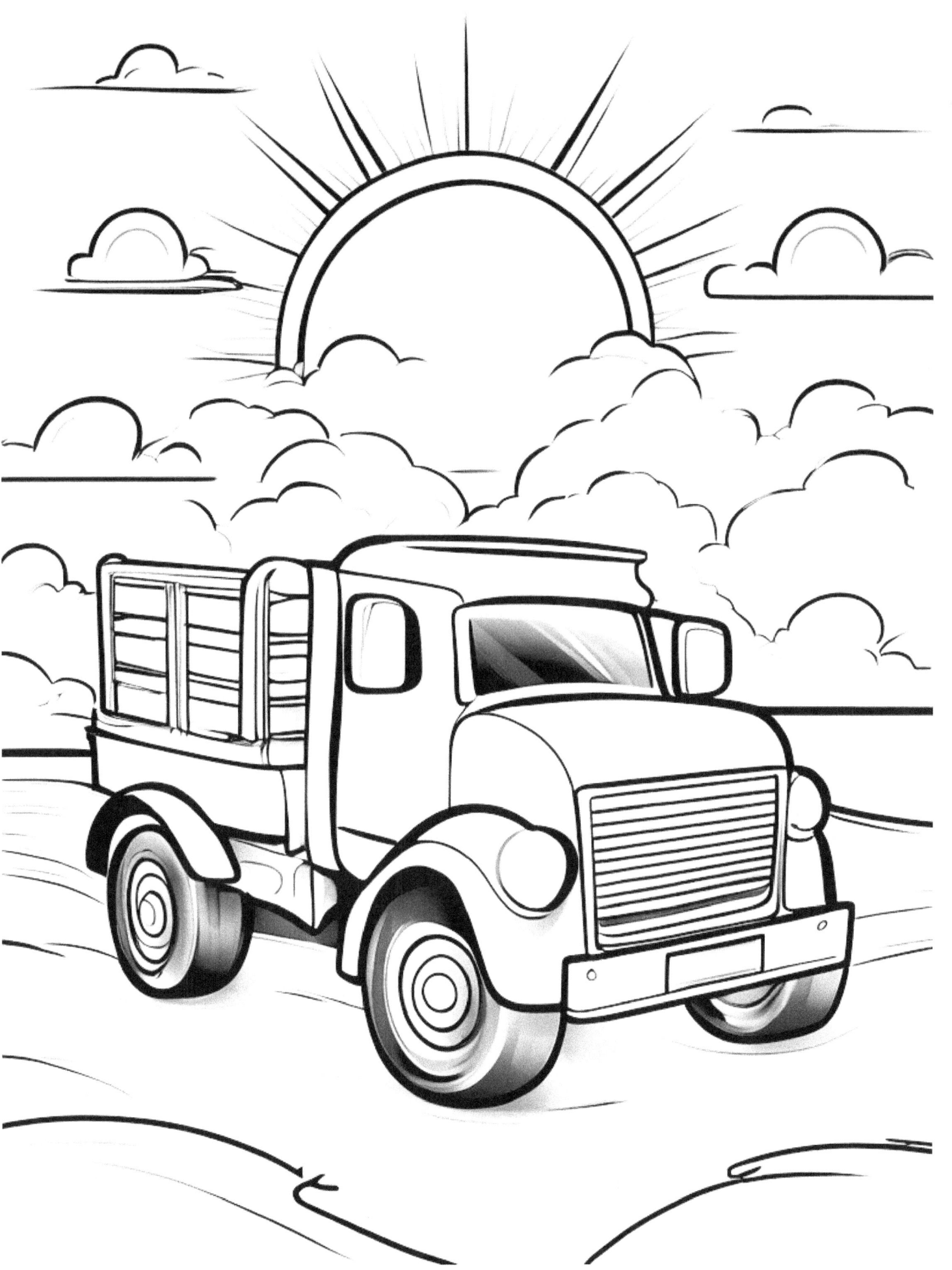

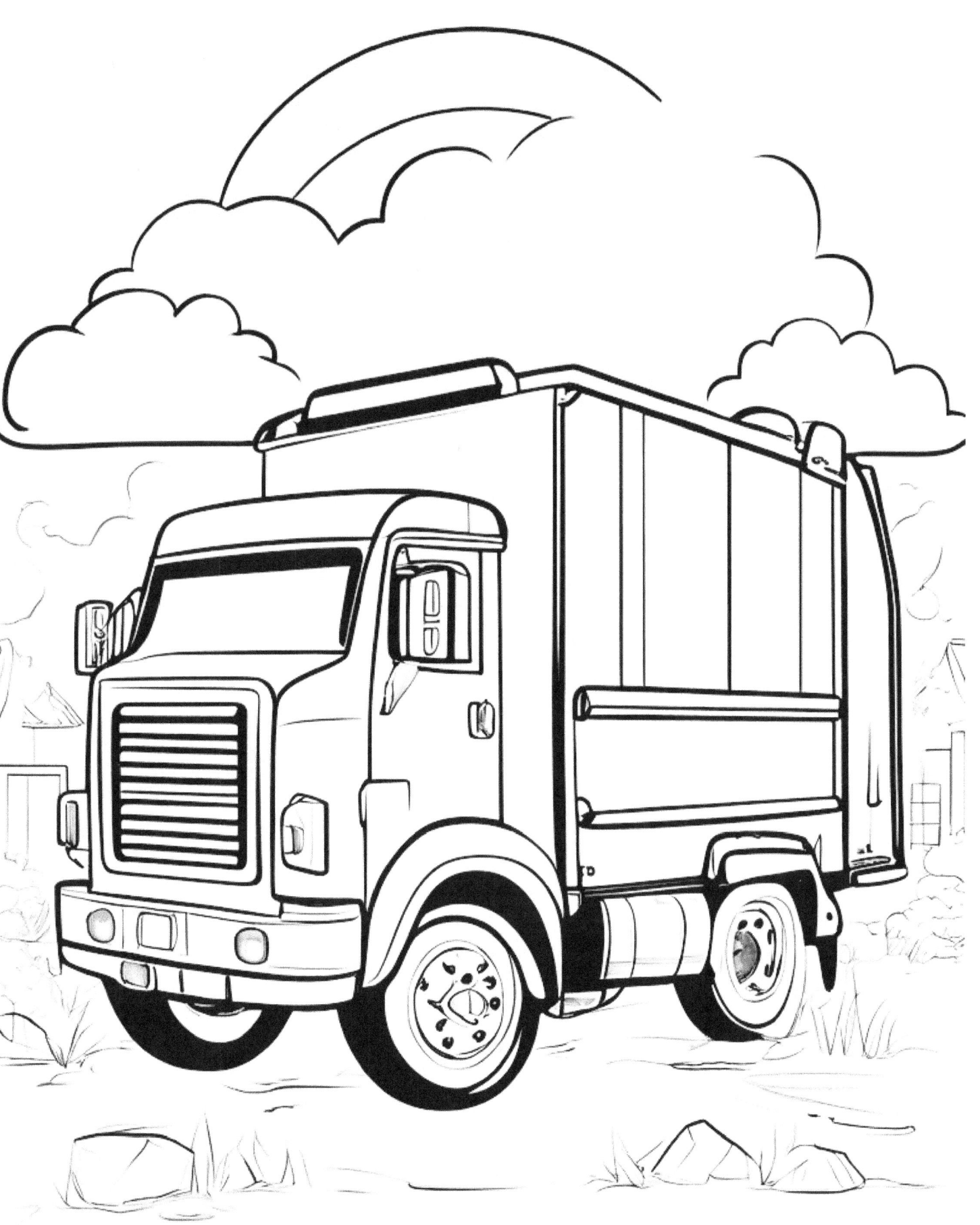

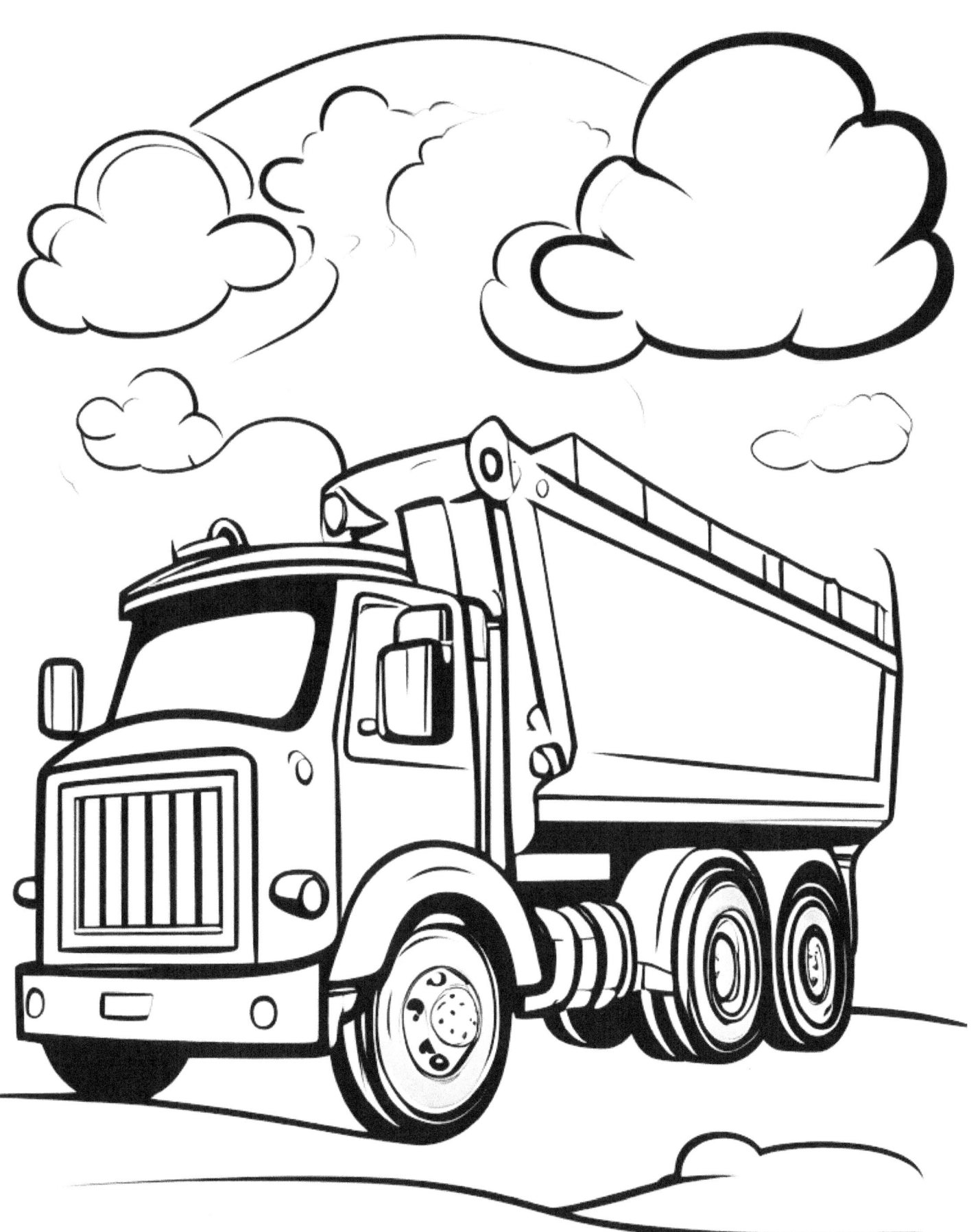

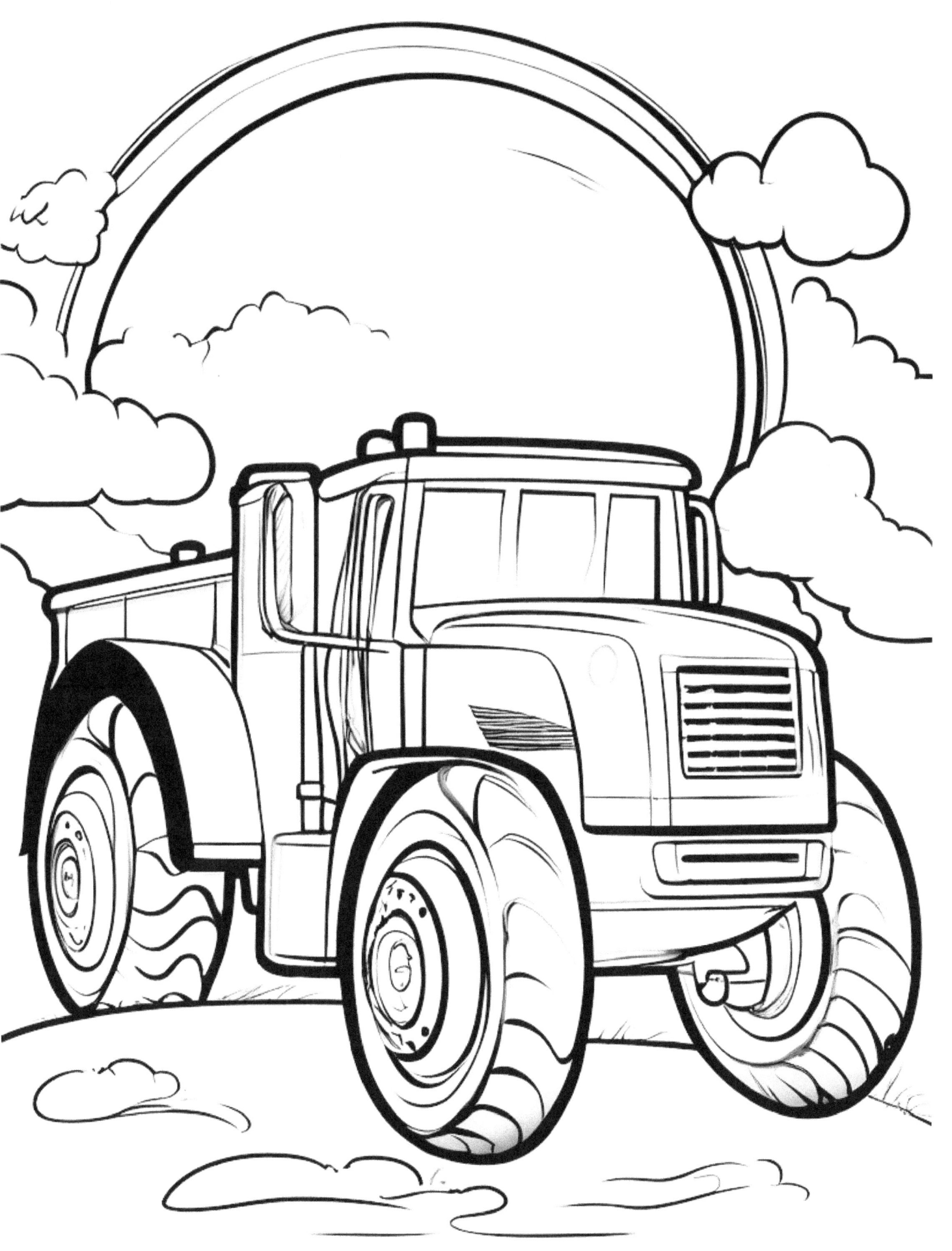

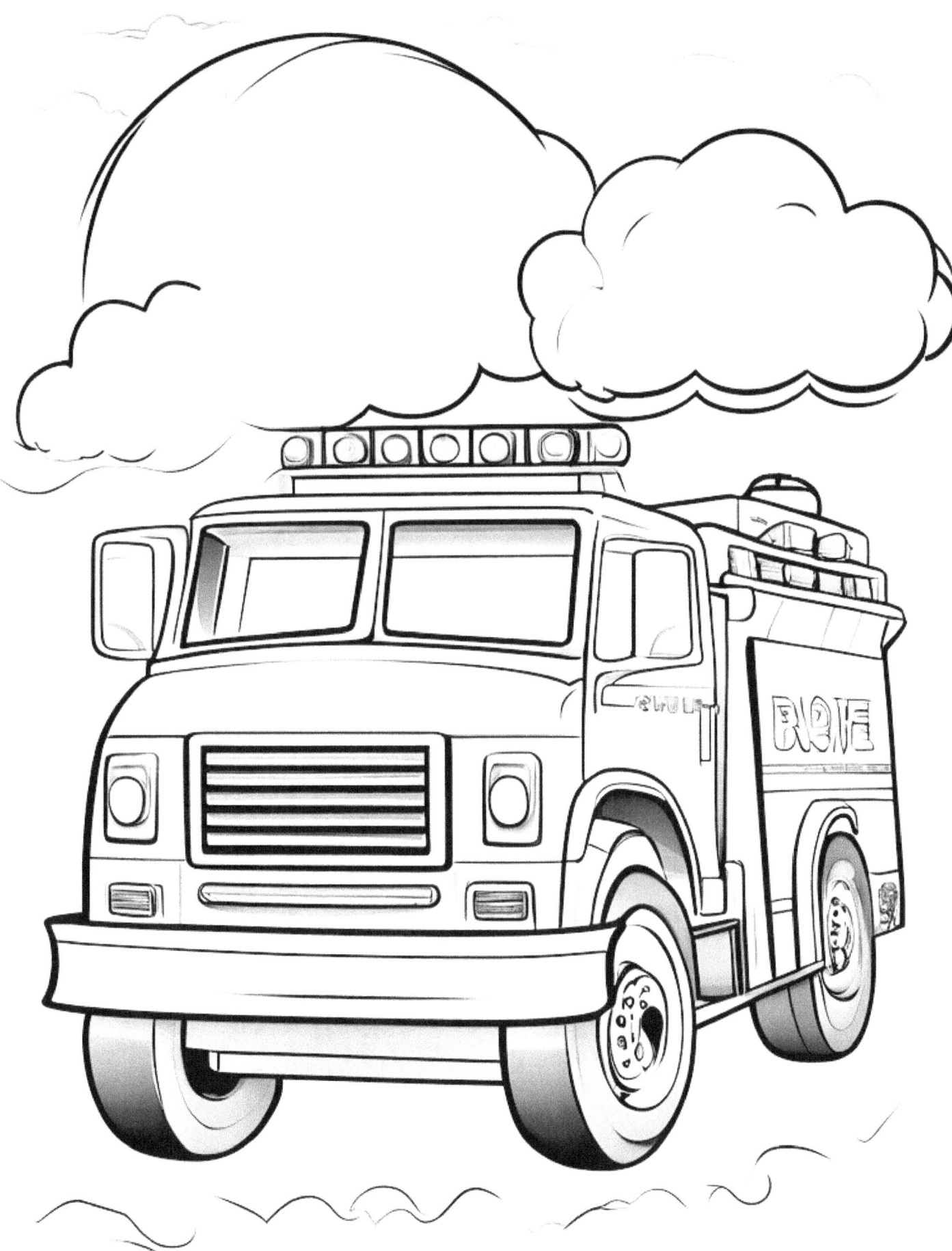

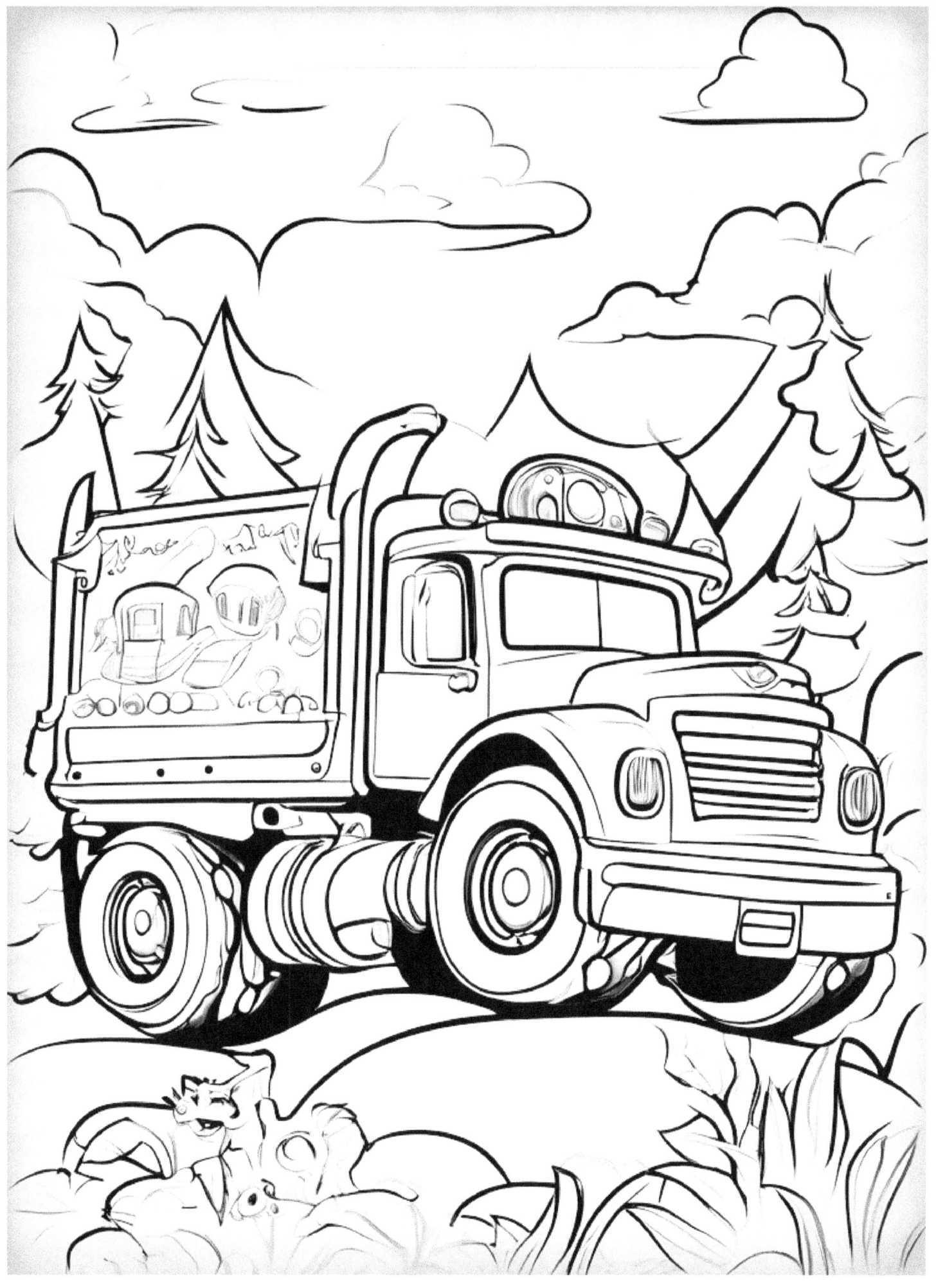

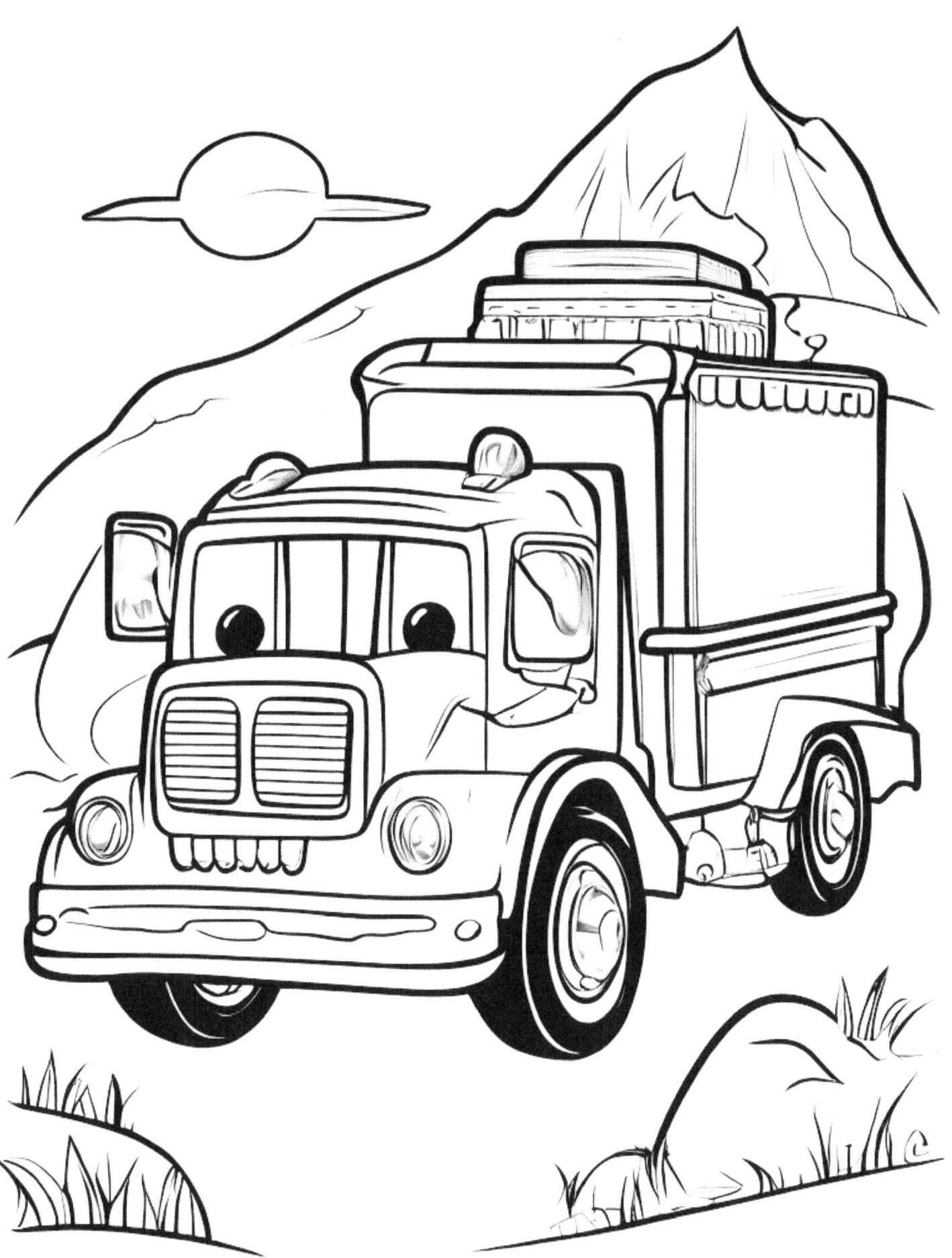

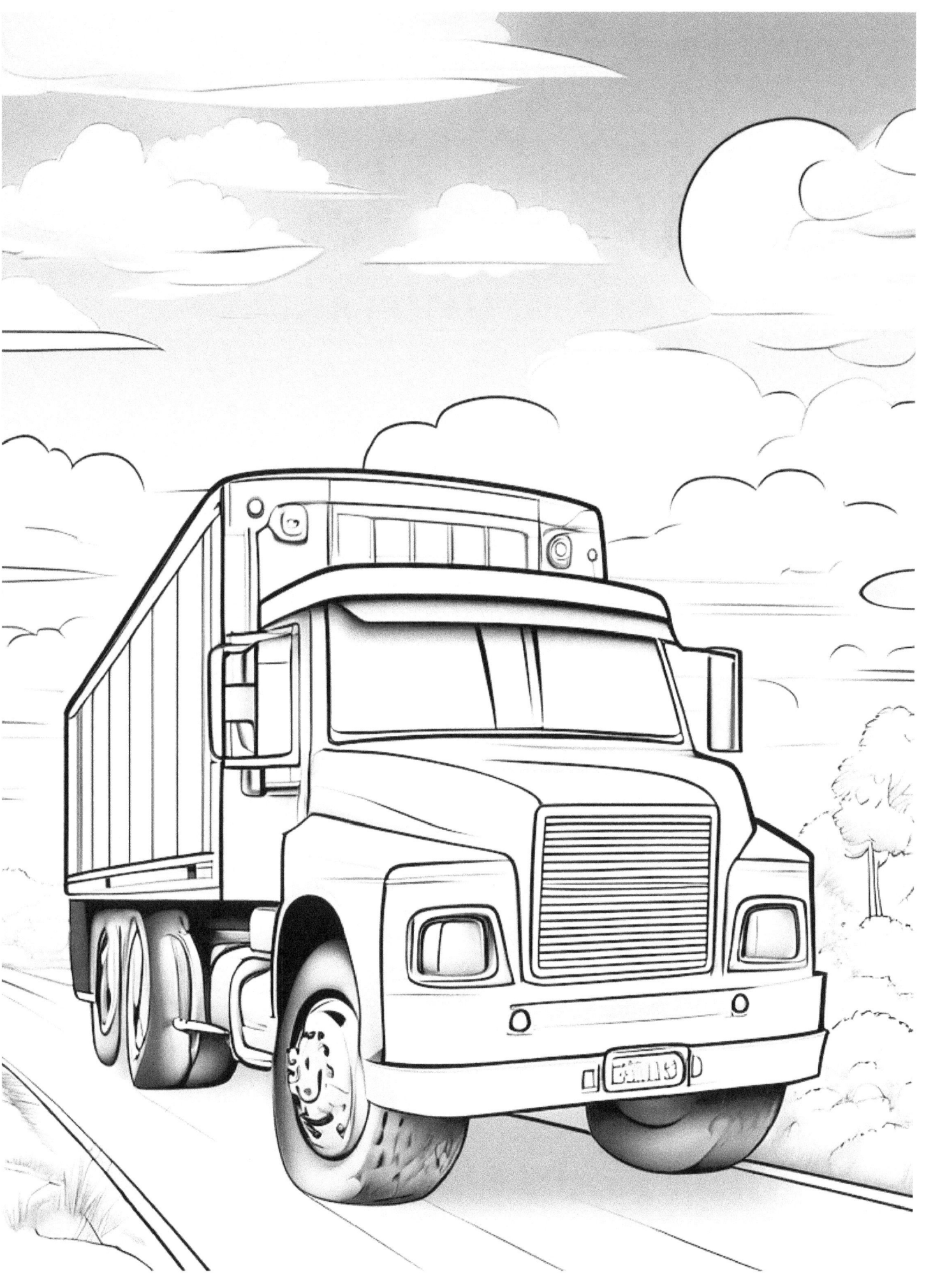

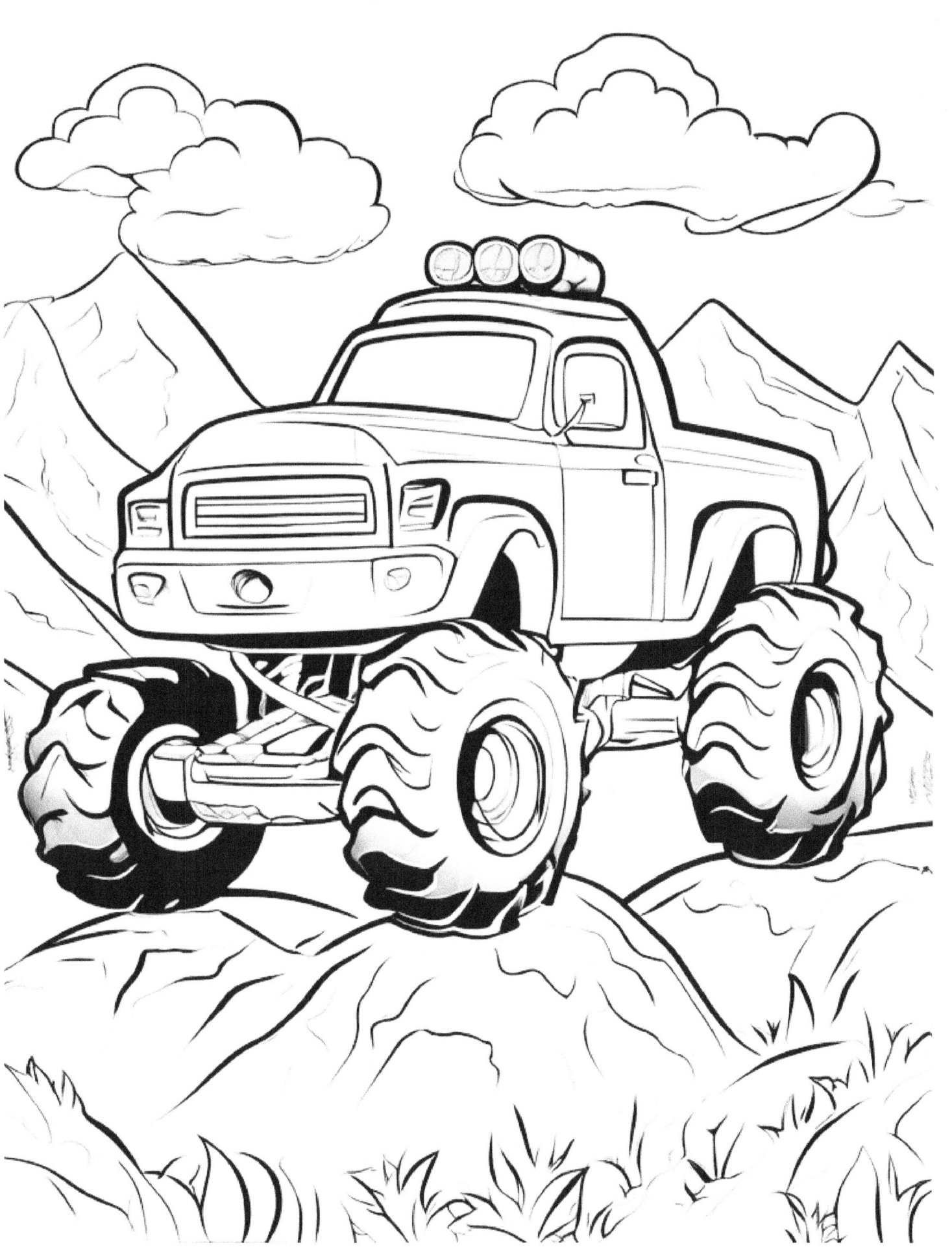

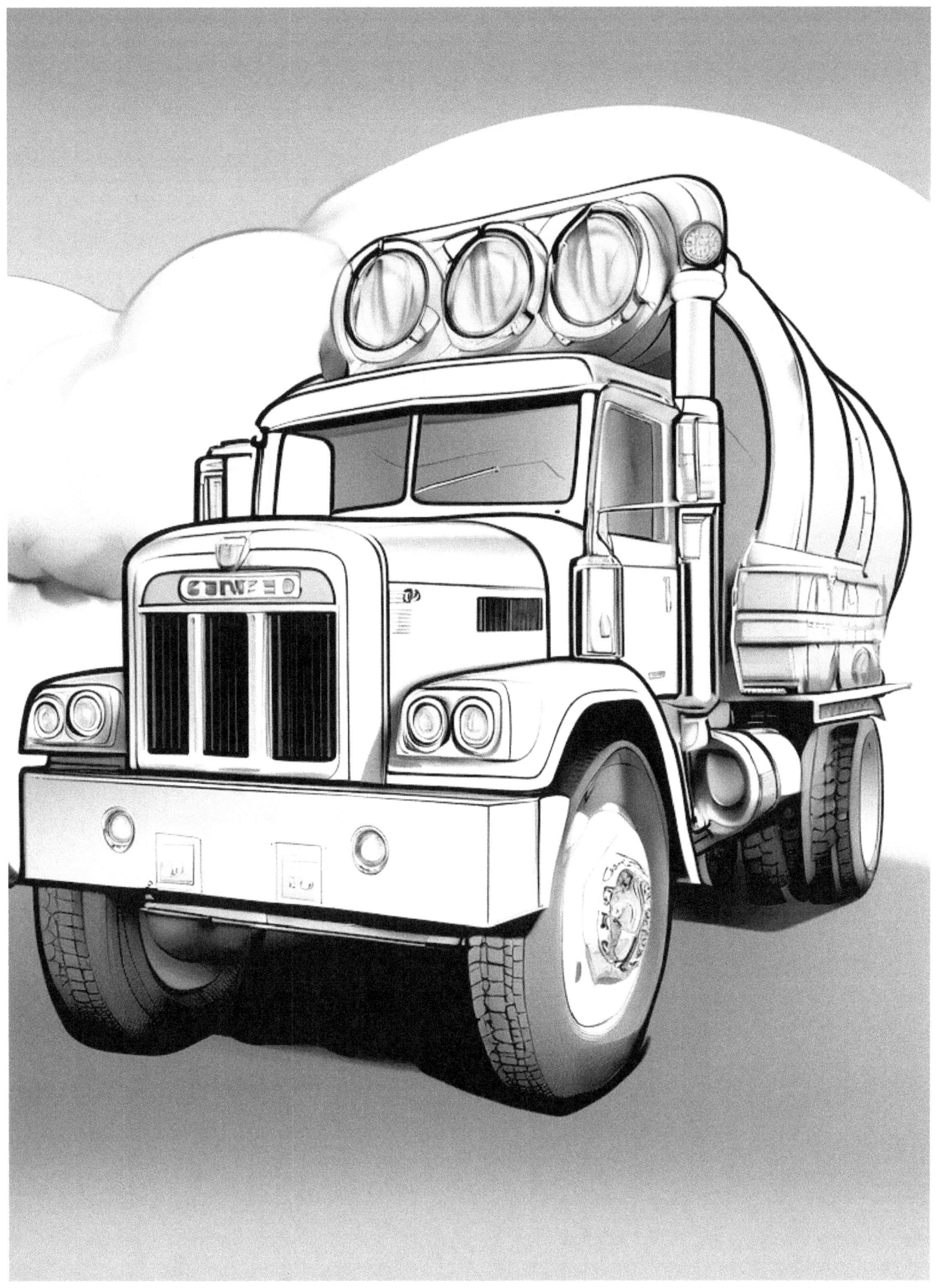

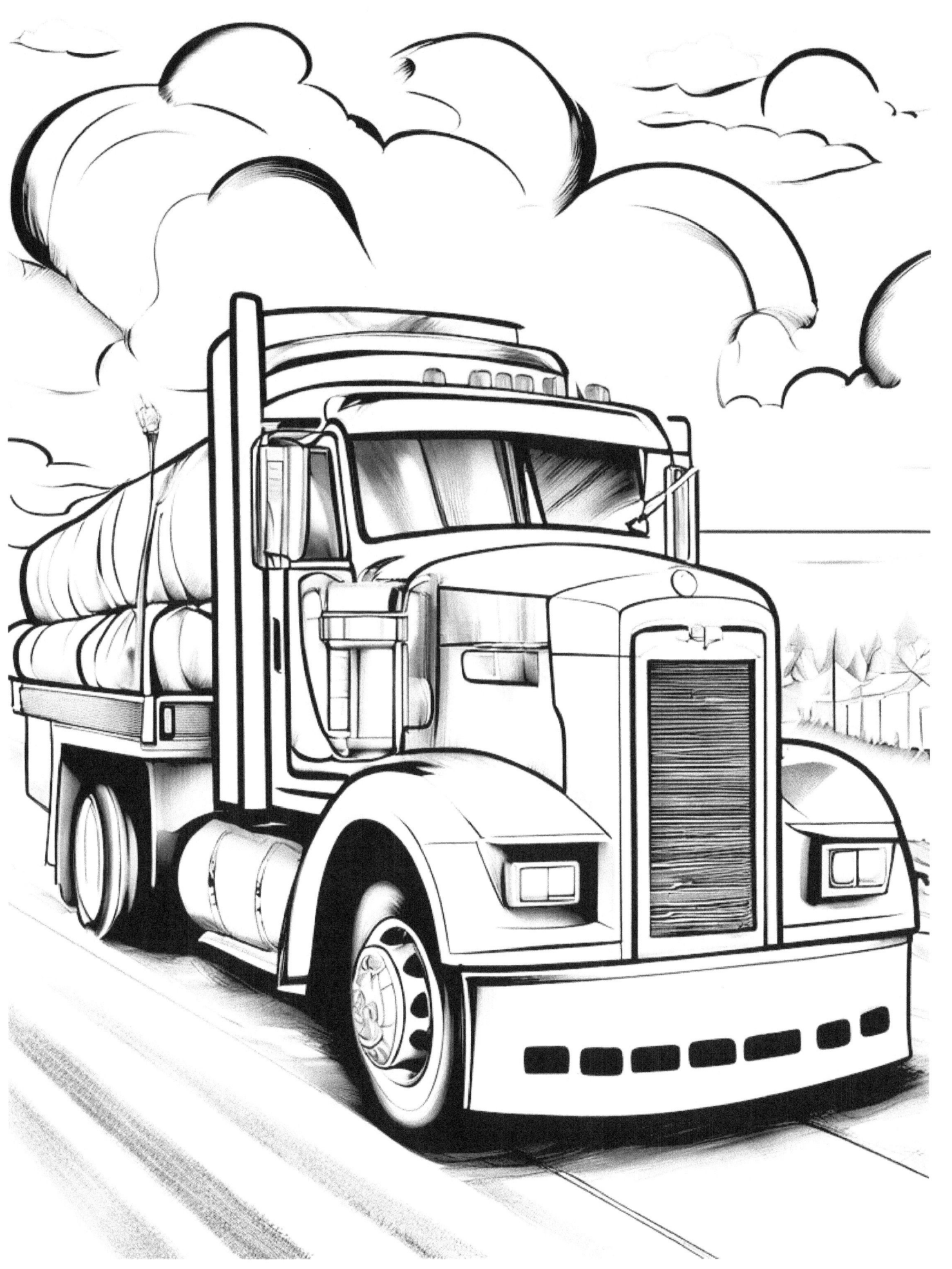

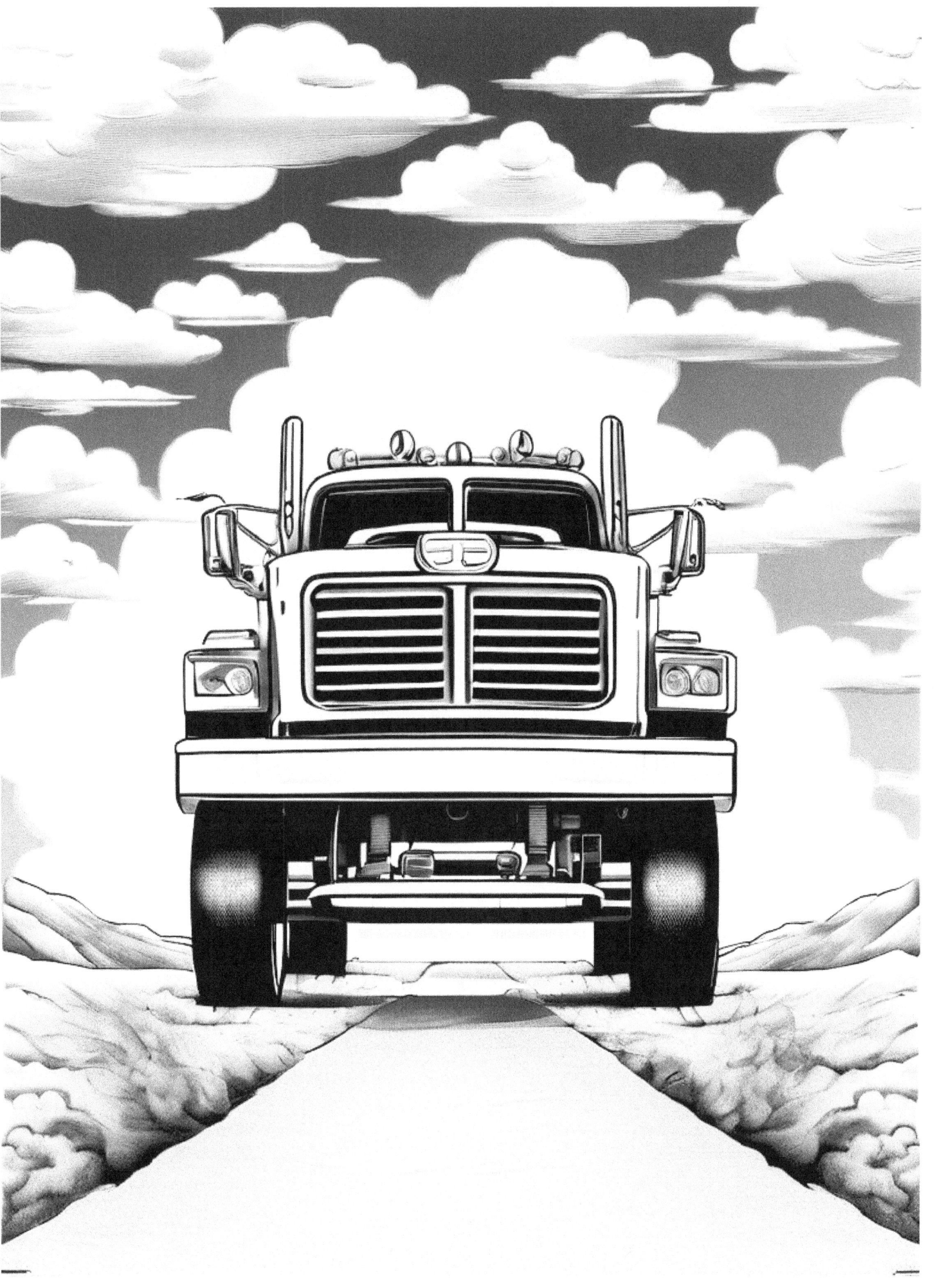

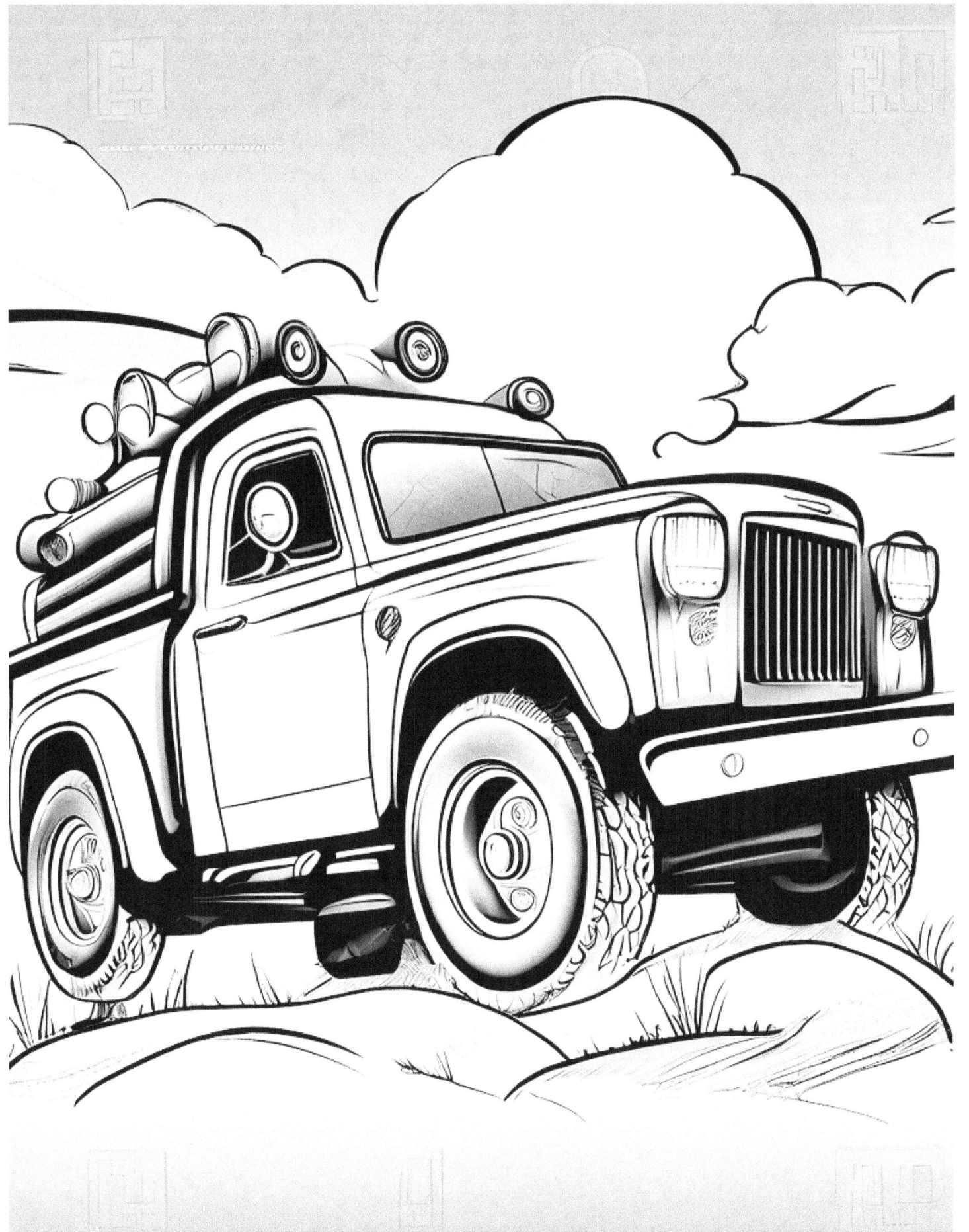

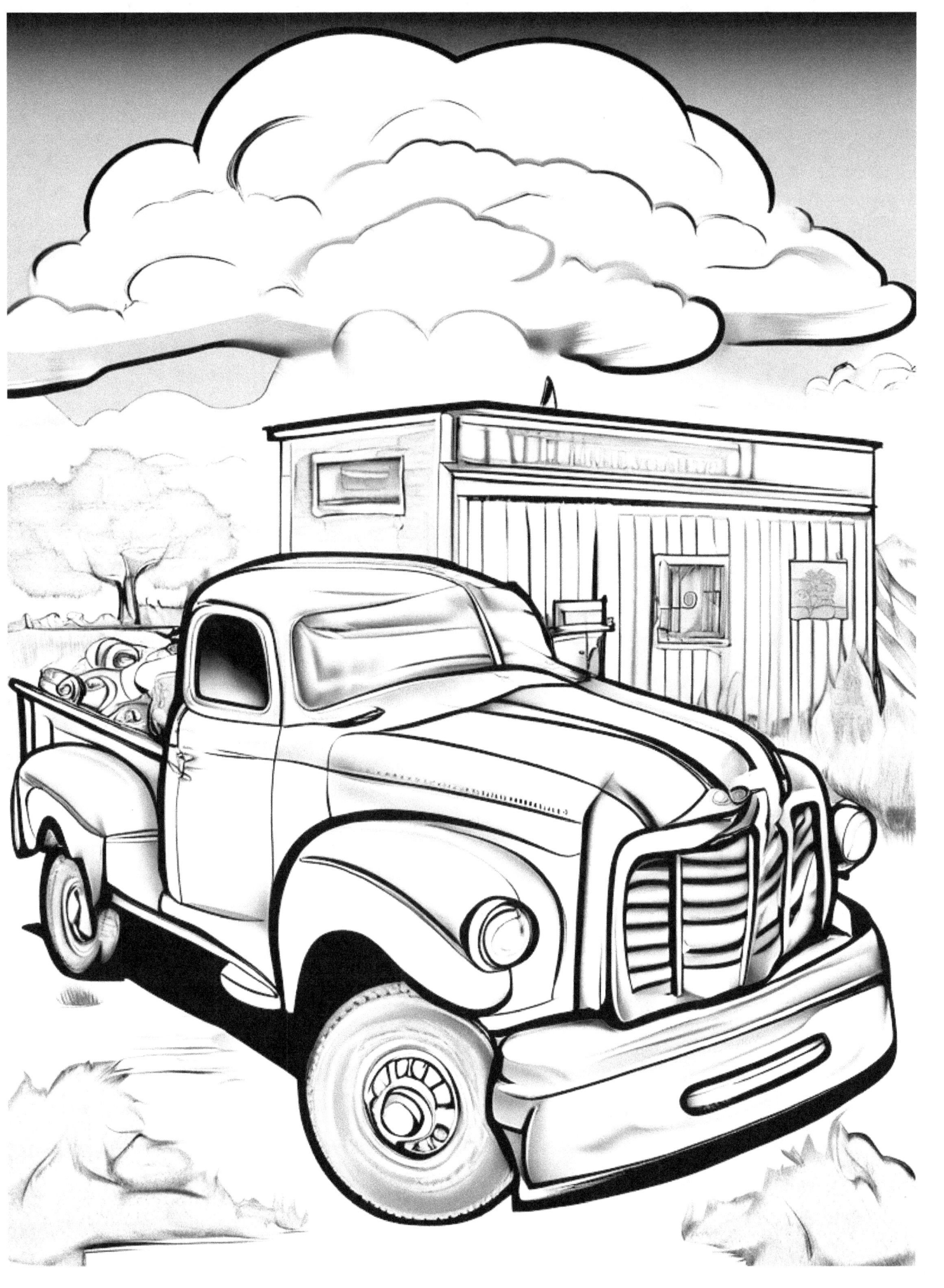

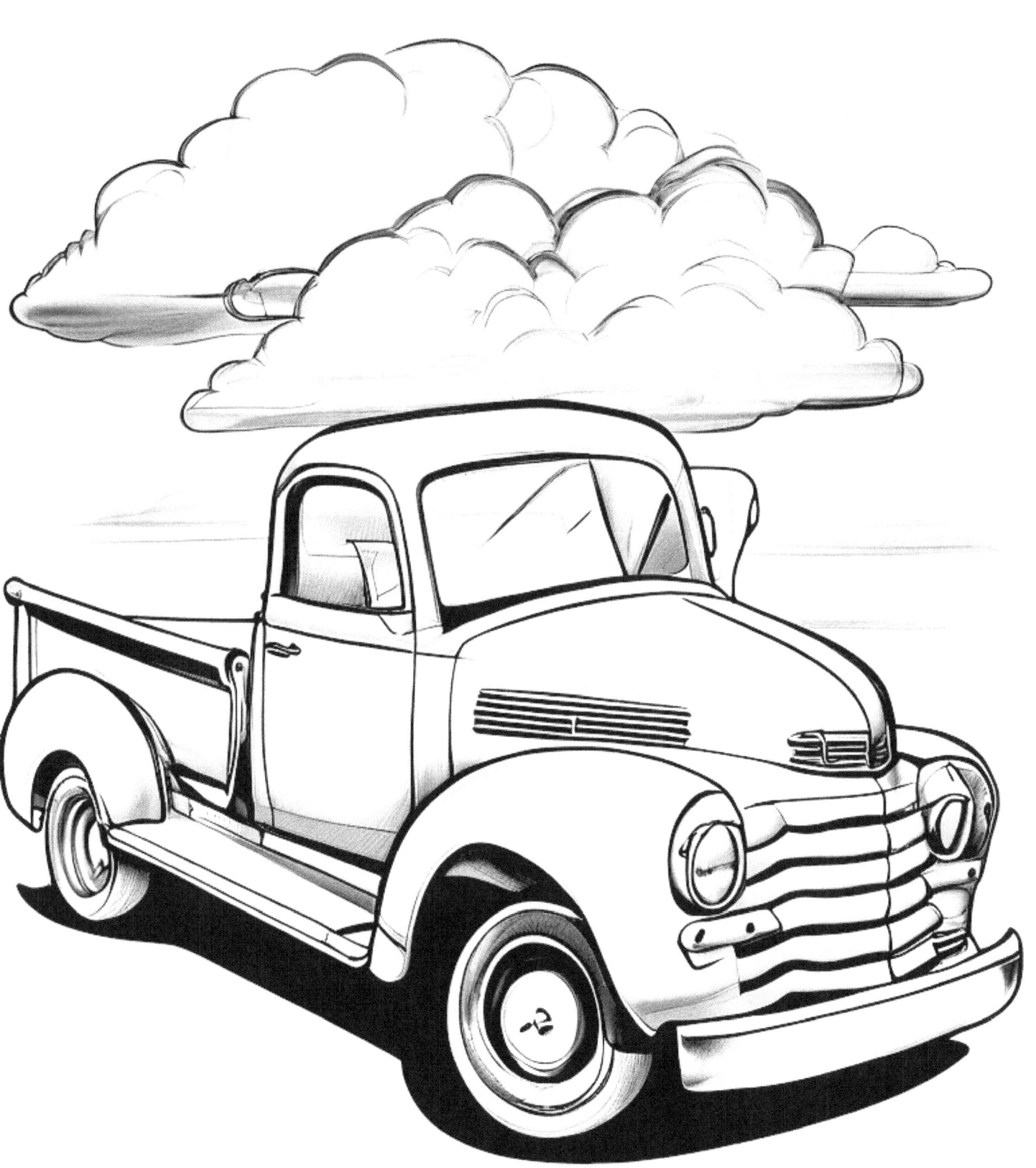

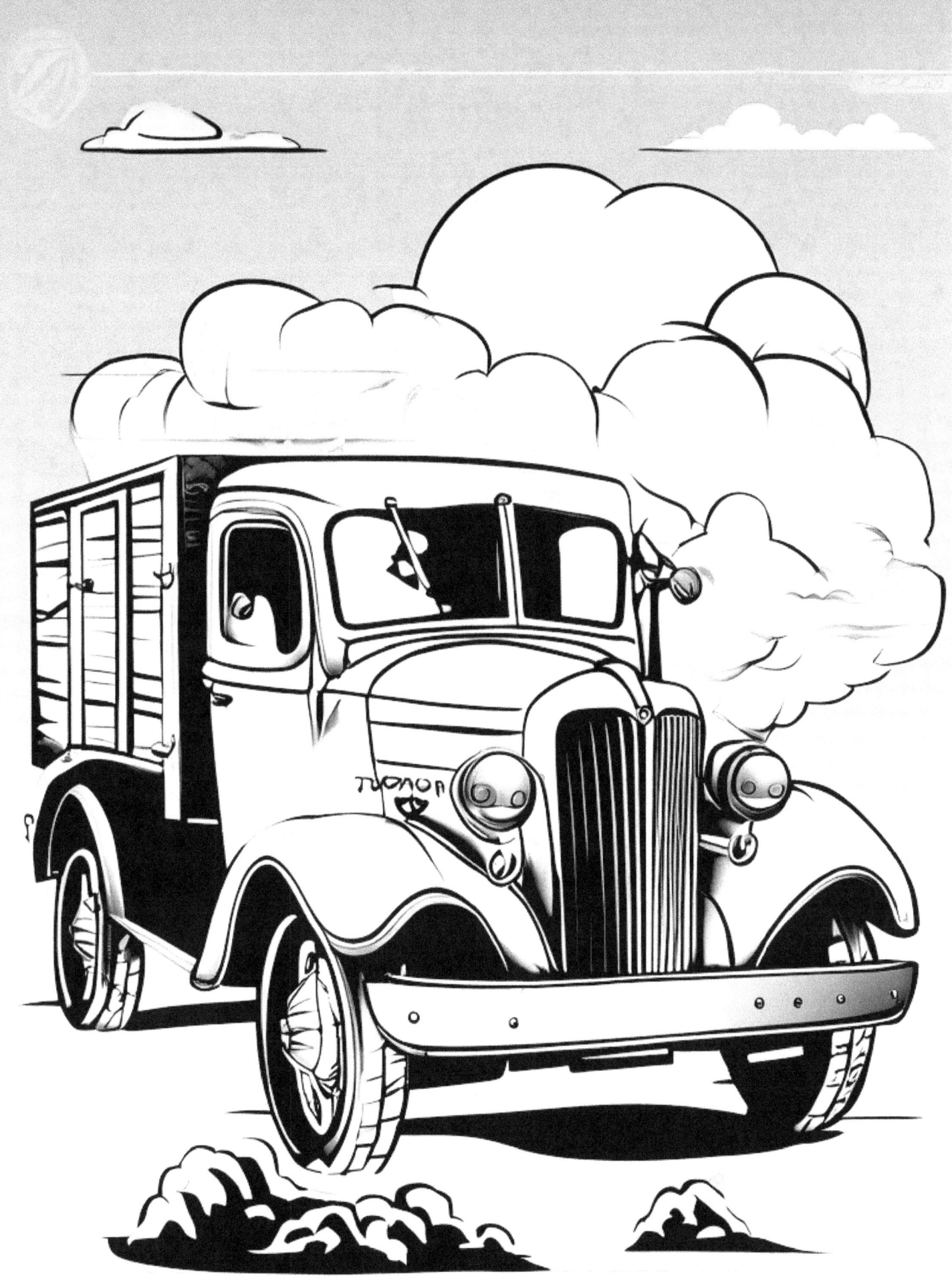

www.ingramcontent.com/pod-product-compliance
Lightning Source LLC
Chambersburg PA
CBHW081136290526
45795CB00006B/2258